D1328662

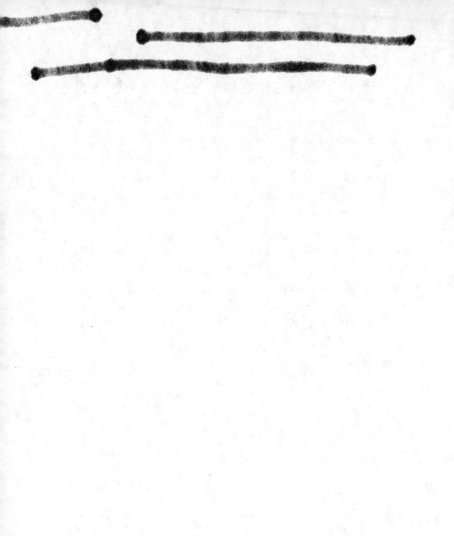

JOB: HIS WIFE, HIS FRIENDS, AND HIS GOD

Donal J O'Connor

Job: His wife, his friends, and his God

the columba press

First edition, 1995, published by
the columba press
93 The Rise, Mount Merrion, Blackrock, Co Dublin

Cover by Bill Bolger
Origination by The Columba Press
Printed in Ireland by Colour Books, Dublin

ISBN 1 85607 127 8

Contents

Author's Preface

The Book of Job is a mighty work of forty-two chapters in difficult
Hebrew, written so long ago (circa 400BC) that many of its linguistic
nuances are no longer discernible. In spite of this hindrance it has
fascinated many translators and commentators, and its image of the
patient Job in the Prologue has strengthened the hearts of sufferers
to bear with perplexing catastrophes; its picture of the angry Job in
the poem, despairing at the injustices and the miseries of human
existence, has influenced the modern literature of the absurd. It has
also influenced painters, engravers, sculptors and musicians, and it
is precisely in this last category that one finds a favourable portrayal
of the wife of Job. Of whom more anon.

The Book of Job deserves a large commentary. Of such there are
several available to the English reader. My work, on the contrary, is
not a commentary; it is a set of seven studies on different topics
central to the tragedy of Job. My first chapter is devoted to the wife
of Job and I have translated the first three chapters of Job to accompany it. My second chapter is on the three friends who came to
comfort Job but failed. To accompany this chapter I have translated
in full the first speech by Eliphaz together with Job's response to it. I
would invite the reader to check out for herself/himself my comments with the biblical text in all cases. Thirdly, then, I moved on to
an analysis of Job's character based, though not exclusively, on his
famous final speech (Chaps 29,30,31). I translated all this speech to
go with the chapter on 'The hybris of Job', and again I invite the
reader to check my views against the biblical text, and to feel free to
formulate alternatives. The author of Job often leaves options open
to his readers.

My fourth chapter, 'A lesson from nature', is devoted to the two
divine speeches (Chaps 38-41), and again I have supplied the biblical text to go with it. The divine speeches are intended to give an
answer to Job's attack on God's justice, and, as such, are at the very
heart of the debate. I have explored various aspects of the divine

speeches in the next chapter (viz. Chap 5). Chapter six looks back over the whole poem to assess Job's changing feelings towards his God. The final chapter is on the prose Epilogue.

In all, I have presented only one third of the total biblical text of Job, because my experience over the years persuades me that the full text, like a full meal, may be too much for some gentle systems to absorb. The intellectual feast of Job is oriental, exotic, with many unusual flavours, sometimes strange to the Western palate.

I refer frequently to the commentary on Job by the late Mgr E.J. Kissane, whose scholarly work deserves to be recalled on the occasion of the bicentenary of the college of which he was a distinguished president. I thank the students who patiently bore with my own initial work on Job while I taught Old Testament in the same college. That was over ten years ago and I have had all those years to delve more fully into the hidden depths of Joban theology. I find, however, that there's more to that great book than I can fathom. But I give what I have found.

Each of the seven chapters can stand by itself, but naturally would be more rewarding if read in sequence together with the appropriate biblical text. The final success of this effort would be if the reader moved on to the full text of Job.

A special word of thanks to the editorial board of the Maynooth Bicentennial Series who invited me to contribute to their celebrations. A sincere thanks to the Irish Theological Quarterly who published my first rather tortuous attempt at a grammatical analysis of Job's Last Word (42:6). I thank ITQ also for permitting a re-edited version of my articles, 'Theodicy in the Whirlwind', 'Reverence and Irreverence in Job'. I thank the late Professor Thomas Marsh who, only two months before his untimely death, read the full text of my manuscript and offered many valuable suggestions. It was on his advice that I added the Glossary.

Glossary

Aramaic: A semitic language similar to Hebrew; it appears in a few parts of the Old Testament. By the time of Jesus Aramaic had replaced Hebrew as the commonly spoken language of Palestine. The influence of Aramaic may be noticed in parts of Job (42:7).

Hebrew: The language of the Old Testament; it has 22 consonants, some of which have no English equivalents, such as ḥ (h with a dot underneath, pronounced like *ch* in the Gaelic *loch*), and the suspended commas in the prepositions *'el* (meaning 'to'), and *'al* (meaning 'upon', 'above', 'concerning') familiar from the logo *El Al* on Israeli airlines. Both commas indicate guttural sounds, and can cause confusion even for the Hebrew scribe in Job 42:7 (see p 156).

The Masoretic Text: The authorised text of the Hebrew Bible, drawn up by Jewish scholars between the sixth and ninth centuries of the Christian era, to preserve uniform spelling and pronunciation.

Targum: A translation of the Hebrew text into Aramaic.

The Septuagint: (The LXX, literally the Seventy,) i.e. the work of the seventy (-two) Jewish scholars who, circa 250BC, translated the Hebrew scriptures into Greek for the benefit of the many Jews in Alexandria and elsewhere who were no longer familiar with Hebrew. As regards the Book of Job, the LXX is shorter than the Masoretic text, but has expansions dealing with the wife of Job. The LXX, widely used in the early Christian church, contained some books not in the Masoretic text.

The Vulgate: (From Latin *vulgata*, 'in common use'.) The famous translation of the Bible by St Jerome, who was requested by Pope Damascus to make a translation of the Old Testament from the Hebrew to replace the Old Latin translation (made from the Greek). Jerome had completed his translation of Job by the year 392, using such Hebrew manuscripts as were available at that time to Jewish scholars.

The Canon of Scripture: The list of books recognised by a religious community as setting out the norm or standard of belief. The word 'canon' comes from the Greek for a reed or norm.

The Jewish Bible consists of 24 books: The Law (the first five books of the bible); the Prophets (eight books in all – counting the twelve minor prophets as one book); the Writings (Psalms, Proverbs, Job etc. – eleven books).

In the Catholic Bible the Old Testament consists of all the books in the Jewish Bible plus seven others: Tobit, Judith, 1 & 2 Maccabees, the Wisdom of Solomon, Sirach (Ecclesiasticus) and Baruch with the Letter of Jeremiah. These seven were already part of the Septuagint scriptures, and are sometimes called deutero-canonical.

In Protestant Bibles the Old Testament contains only those books which form the Jewish Bible, but in a different order and enumeration, yielding 39 books. Some Protestant Bibles include the seven deutero-canonicals under the name *Apocrypha*.

Introduction

The Book of Job is one of the world's greatest and most perplexing masterpieces. It consists of a story and a dialogue. The first, in prose, is quite brief: in chapters 1 and 2, often called the Prologue, the Satan asks whether Job would persevere in his piety if all his prosperity were to be replaced by evil. When Job is reduced to dust and ashes by Satan, he continues to bless God and so proves that disinterested piety is humanly possible.

The second part, the dialogue, is a long poem (Chaps 3-41) and its conclusion more uncertain. There are six speakers in this debate, viz. Job himself, now no longer patient, who accuses God of injustice; his three friends who defend the thesis that a person's sufferings are a divine punishment for his sins; a young man, Elihu who enters uninvited after the friends have given up and, in Chaps 33-37, gives his view that Job's sufferings are medicinal, leading him back to God. (Neither Job, nor his friends, nor the deity take any notice of Elihu). Finally the Lord himself speaks from the whirlwind (Chaps 38-41), and Job accepts the divine words (42:1-6).

This great poem is followed by a prose Epilogue in the naïve style of the Prologue, and gives a happy ending with Job restored by God to his former happiness. All's well that ends well!

The author has set his characters at least a thousand years earlier than his own time. Resemblances with the patriarchal narratives in Genesis are striking; both Abraham and Job depend on cattle and servants for their well-being. And both Job and Abraham were father-figures of outstanding piety who were severely tested by God, to see if, under great adversity, they would persevere in their loyalty to God. Abraham did (Gen 22), and so did Job (1, 2).

Thus from the very outset we see that great suffering and the early death of children need not be interpreted as divine punishment for sin, as the friends thought.

We the readers, have, by special courtesy of the author of the Book of Job, been granted audience to the heavenly council and we know that Job is being 'tested', not punished for any hypothetical sins. But neither Job nor his friends have been given this information. If they had, there would be no Book of Job as we know it.

There might, instead, be a debate on whether Job's severe 'testing' was worthy of a benign deity.

Job's God

Job's view of God is not something fixed and static throughout. Job adopts at least four different viewpoints, seeing God differently at different stages of his long spiritual journey from prosperity to despair.

At first (1, 2) Job, in the days of his prosperity, sees God as the giver of all the good gifts of life: material possessions, numerous family and personal happiness. Job honours God and is observant of all due ritual. When great catastrophes eventually reduce him to nothingness he patiently accepts evil from the hand of God: the Lord who gave has now taken away; may the name of the Lord be blessed. Job does not regard his sorrows as a punishment for any sin, nor did he regard his former prosperity as a reward for his piety. He does not subscribe to the view, sometimes held in religious circles, that all suffering is a punishment for sin. Both the author of the Book of Job and the deity concede that Job, both before and after his troubles, remained loyal to God, in unquestioning simple faith.

This unquestioning faith of the Prologue gives way to darker angry emotions in the poem, beginning with chapter 3 right up to chapter 12, where irreverence towards God touches on blasphemy. See especially *Reverence and Irreverence* below.

In chapter 3 Job, without blaming God, voices his despair at his own sad life and wishes he were dead. In Chapter 7 he goes a step further and is openly disrespectful to God, seeing God as condemning mankind (and not just Job) to the cruel life of a concentration camp of forced labour. (Note the term 'hard labour' – Hebrew *Zabha'* in 7:1; conscripted forced labour was common in King Solomon's time and afterwards.) Job now is sufficiently self-analytical to realise that his language is outrageous and that his anti-God outbursts arise from the anguish of his disturbed mind (7:11). In this mood he asserts that God only mocks the innocent man at his trial (9:23). From God no justice can be expected. Finally, God is not only unjust to Job, but to humanity generally because the whole mess of human society, with its corruption in high places, judicial maladministration, the inevitable oppression of the poor by the rich, is ultimately God's responsibility (12).

A further development in Job's view of God takes place in chapter 13 and continues right to the end of Job's great soliloquy (27-31). The deep irreverence against an unjust God gives way to a search for someone who would present Job's case fairly before the divine tribunal and win him an acquittal. This new mood of hope makes sense only against the background of the legal process which, from Solomon's time down to the end of the monarchy, was available to a private citizen who felt unjustly treated by the crown administration (in matters of conscripted labour, military service, taxation, and also in some matters of criminal law – see M. Elon, *The Principles of Jewish Law*, Jerusalem 1974, 30).

Just as in a modern monarchy the case of a private citizen versus the crown does not necessarily imply the citizen's personal hostility towards the sovereign, so Job's complaint against God, in his plea for a lawsuit (Hb. *Rib*) against God, does not imply his turning against God. See the text of 31:35-37 for Job's last word – a word, not of despair, but of hope for justice from God when, eventually, someone (of the heavenly council?) is deputed to hear his case in the name of the Almighty.

Job's fourth and final view of God comes only at the very end, 42:1-6 (See Text). It is a prayer of wonder at the power and wisdom of the Creator. It is also a prayer to the mystery of God which is beyond human understanding. On divine justice and mercy, however, Job is silent. He only speaks of what he knows from his own sad experience.

Job retracts his rash words spoken during his illness, but the Lord didn't fault him on any sins prior to that, and so his sufferings need not be attributed to any hypothetical sins. Job's fault was not in the sphere of morality but in that of wisdom. The Lord respected the conscience of Job, and so Job can address God in prayer.

> 'I had heard of you with the hearing of the ear,
> But now my eye sees you' (42:5).

Job's friends

The three friends have been the object of much criticism both from Job himself and a host of commentators who, over the centuries, have taken Job's side in the debate. It is impossible to summarise the friends' case, for the good reason that the three are quite different in their approach to Job.

In Eliphaz's opening speech (4, 5) he has high praise for Job's many good qualities and sees these as affording hope for his recovery. Only the wicked, he asserts, are completely forsaken by God, and Job is not in that category. In his third speech, however, Eliphaz changes his position and declares Job 'a very wicked man' (22:5), and so deserving of divine chastisement; his only hope now is to banish wrongdoing from his life (22:23).

Even if the friends err in attributing Job's sufferings to his supposed sinfulness, they nevertheless contribute to the debate by their realistic appraisal of man's moral and physical weakness. Job, in his two long poems of self-praise (29, 31) never admits to a moral fault, and, of course, the Prologue had presented him as a perfect man. For the friends, however, there is no such thing on this earth as a perfect man. Man, made from the earth, is a fragile creature, like a piece of pottery, easily broken (4:19). Pestilence and disease are endemic in the earth from which mankind is made (5:7), so that man is 'loathsome and laps up evil like water' (15:16). Eliphaz, who is the speaker in all these texts, is speaking of all mankind (including Job); even if they have many good deeds to their credit, they may still be drawn into the all-pervasive evil of the world. In the case of a deliberate offence, the sinner must repent and banish wrongdoing from his house (22:23). See the chapter on Job's comforters.

While Eliphaz is urbane, Bildad must seem to us deeply offensive with his unsubstantiated charge that all Job's children were sinners who deserved their cruel death (8:4). He probably inferred from their early demise that they must have sinned seriously. But what is important about Bildad's case is his contrasting the fate of the children with that of Job: Job is a good man whom God will one day restore to happiness (8:20-22).

Bildad is a man for facts: Job's children are dead; Job is alive. He is also a man for interpreting facts: Job's children must have been sinners; Job is not a sinner. So there is strong hope for Job's recovery, because it is the wicked not the just that are punished by God. Bildad therefore hopes that his words will bring comfort to Job.

When God sees a good person suffering seriously over a long period, why does he not intervene? To those Israelites who were the first readers of the Book of Job, three possible answers sprang to mind: Job is being tested, not to find out if he has already sinned, but to see if, in extreme adversity, he would persevere in his piety. (The reader, but not Job and friends, have been told this in chapters one and two); secondly, Job is being tortured 'without cause', to borrow the phrase used in 2:3. Job, in such a case, would be like the other innocent suffers celebrated in well-known poems of the ancient world from Egypt to Mesopotamia. Take one example: the poem *ludlul bel nemeqi* ('I will praise the Lord of Wisdom'), also referred to as 'The Poem of the Righteous Sufferer', composed in the second millenium before the Christian era.

The hero of this poem was stricken with a disease for over a year. He prayed to his god and goddess for deliverance from his illness but they did not answer him. He had always observed the ways of piety and never neglected religious rites – he has no sins really, and his only prayer is not for forgiveness but for deliverance. Eventually his prayer is answered and he is restored to health.

Now Eliphaz's advice in his first and second speeches is that Job should appeal to God for deliverance; there is no suggestion that Job has deliberately committed sin, and therefore any prayer of Job's need be not for forgiveness but for deliverance. The fact that Eliphaz, when he comes to his third speech, changes his opinion about Job's integrity and now accuses him of specific sins, should not blind the reader to the more benign approaches of his earlier speeches.

When we listen to the third friend, Zophar, we hear for the first time the clear statement of Job's sinfulness: 'Know that God is exacting from you less than your sin deserves' (11:6c). This one short sentence may stun us with its absolute insensitivity to the plight of the suffering Job who could hardly be more miserable. And still, like Bildad's famous one-liner about Job's children deserving their cruel death, Zophar intends to console Job by the implication that, even in Job's sufferings, God's mercy is at work. God has mercifully spared Job the full punishment due to his sins, and this fact, says Zophar, should give Job hope that the same divine mercy will restore him to happiness once more. Zophar, like Bildad and Eliphaz, sees himself as 'Job's comforter'. All three finish their arguments with hope for Job's recovery. Job, however, rejects their words. His view is that God as the supreme ruler of the world should act according to the norms of justice and answer the plea of the innocent who cries out to him for protection. He is sure that if he could get a fair hearing at the divine tribunal God would vindicate him – not a question of forgiveness for sins but vindication of a just cause.

But there is a third possible explanation for the sufferings of a good person, and Eliphaz, according to Kissane, seems to favour this line in chapter 4. Although in chapter 15 Eliphaz will accuse Job of deliberate evil, in chapter 4 he doesn't go as far as that, but restricts himself to sins committed inadvertently. Even a good man may, at times, because of human frailty, lapse into evil without realising it. In such a case he should accept with patience the temporary

discipline which the Almighty inflicts on him and hope for forgiveness and recovery.

Which of these three possible 'explanations' fits in with the
friends' case? We can eliminate the first (the 'testing' hypothesis)
which features in the Prologue, but never on the lips of the friends.
The hypothesis of Job's sufferings being a punishment for his sins
(be they deliberate or indeliberate) is clearly stated for the first time
in Zophar's opening speech (chapter 11), and is adopted by the
other two friends later. But what of Eliphaz and Bildad in their
opening speeches? Do they regard Job as a good man who is suffering 'without cause' and whose best course is to cry out to God to
'rouse' himself to deliver the afflicted? (We may recall Psalms 35
and 44 where the innocent sufferer becomes impatient with God's
delay in delivering him; Job himself adopts such an approach.) The
question receives no clear answer in the opening speeches of
Eliphaz and Bildad. The author of Job is leaving the matter open,
and this is part of the subtlety of the debate.

Job's wife

The Book of Job reflects very much a man's world, in which all the
participants in the long theological debate are males. Only one
woman speaks, and she has only one sentence in the whole drama
(2:9). The author doesn't even tell us her name, or what became of
her afterwards, except that she is the wife of Job. The one sentence
she speaks is nearly always translated to give a blasphemous intent:
'Curse God and die'. Not only the Christian Fathers but most commentators, ancient and modern, paint a very black picture of this
lady. In my chapter on 'The wife of Job' I have, perhaps unwisely,
taken a more benign view of her, and translated her famous words
as an invitation to her husband to continue to 'Bless God'.

One feature of the Book of Job is the author's subtlety in formu-
lating different approaches by each of the six disputants and his
deliberate exploration of the enigmas and ambiguities of life and of
language. Thus, the very last verse of the poem (42:6) can be interpreted either as Job's repentance for his rash language against God,
or as his being comforted in his sufferings by God's speaking to him
at long last and enlightening him on his problem. The author, I suggest, is being deliberately enigmatic.

His subtlety has resulted in causing even the best commentators
to disagree heartily among themselves not merely on individual
words but on central issues: Do the three friends regard Job as
wicked? Edward J. Kissane (*The Book of Job*, Dublin, 1939) says No,
whereas Marvin H. Pope (*Job*, New York, 1965, 36) gives an emphatic

Yes, and castigates Kissane's view as 'casuistry surpassing that of the friends'. My own attempt to propose a compromise between these two scholars has been given above. The reader may wish to investigate this in examining the text of Eliphaz's first speech (4, 5) and Job's response to it (6, 7). (The author of Job, like James Joyce, has kept the professors guessing.)

A feature of the Book of Job is that not just the biblical scholars are drawn into the exploration game but that sometimes a gifted literary artist with no competence in ancient Hebrew may hit the nail on the head, as Muriel Spark did in her Joban novel, *The Only Problem*, when she spotted the use of the 'domestic we' in Job's reply to his wife (2:10).

I have given a translation of all of the first three chapters of Job, so that the reader can see for herself/himself the full text and the two possible translations of 2:9 (where Job's wife speaks). I promise to bear no ill-will towards any reader who prefers the traditional 'dim' view of Job's wife.

The one sentence spoken by Job's wife is like the small pebble cast into the tranquil pond which sends ripples to its farthest limits. I have given a small sampling of these ripples from the great commentators. The lady deserves a second hearing. The author of Job, who belongs to the Wisdom tradition with its fascination for riddles and difficult sayings has, I suggest, deliberately left an option to the reader in 2:9.

While the figure of the suffering Job has had an enormous impact on writers, ancient and modern, we have to turn to the visual arts to find the wife of Job. In the world of ballet, Ninette de Valois' *Job: a Masque for Dancing in Eight Scenes* (1930); stone carvings in Chartres Cathedral (c.1255 AD) showing Job's wife grieving for him; Albrecht Dürer's Jabach altarpiece with Job's wife, beautifully dressed, washing her husband's sore-filled flesh; George de la Tour's (seventeenth century) painting in Epinal showing a youngish wife in long pink robe, holding a lighted candle while she looks down with concern at her stricken husband; and finally William Blake's set of twenty-two engravings for the Book of Job, in twenty-one of which he portrays the faithful wife of Job, so close physically and emotionally to her husband. In Blake's seventh engraving she is almost the Pieta figure of the Virgin supporting the body of Jesus on her lap. Blake (1757-1827) who was not only a master engraver but a poet of vision and daring, has seen the wife of Job in a nobler vein than any artist before him.

It is to this chorus of choreographers, sculptors, painters and engravers that I tune my lyre in chapter one.

Note

For a fuller Introduction see David J.A. Clines, *Job 1-20*, Word Biblical Commentary, Dallas, 1989. See review of same in *ITQ*, 56 (1990) 4, 336-338. Part Two of this large and sensitive commentary is due in 1995. We will then have to count its pages to see if it is larger than the *Moralia* on Job by Pope Gregory the Great.

CHAPTER 1

The wife of Job and anti-feminism

There is only one sentence in the whole Book of Job spoken by a woman, and that woman is the wife of Job, and the mother of the ten children who have been cruelly killed while they were all enjoying a party together. She speaks her mind briefly and her one sentence (2:9) keeps resounding in our memory long after the long speeches of Job and his friends have faded away.

There are two different ways of interpreting this one sentence. Most modern translations show a wife inciting her devoutly religious husband to turn his back on God; they translate the wife's word (in Hebrew *Barek*, literally 'bless') as a euphemism for 'curse'. A second possibility, however, is to take a benign view, so to speak, and regard the wife as urging her husband to continue in his piety, to bless God, and die in that prayerful attitude. This second view is so rare that I leave it aside for the moment and try to explore the implications of the generally accepted translation of her statement, in which she uttered the most daring sentence in the whole Bible. She says to Job:

'Do you still persevere in your integrity? Curse God, and die.' (2:9)

Her outburst must be seen in the context of the three horrific blows that the Adversary ('Satan'), had, with divine permission, inflicted on her household: the destruction of all their property, the death of all her ten children, and finally the serious and humiliating illness of her husband. Before this final blow fell on Job he had shown great patience in adversity in a little poem that has served many afflicted souls in their hour of sorrow, even when no hope of recovery can be seen on the horizon:

'Naked I came forth from my mother's womb, and naked shall I return there. The Lord has given, The Lord has taken away. May the name of the Lord be blessed'. (1:21)

In all this time, Job's wife made no protest against her husband's patient acceptance of God's will. But when the final blow fell on him, when she saw her husband, his whole body covered with sores, sitting as an outcast on the ashes, she immediately spoke up for the first and only time. Then she reproached her husband for his meek acceptance of God's cruel ways.

Here then are two people, husband and wife, faced with the extermination of their entire family in what we would now call a Holocaust situation. There are only two possible responses to their situation: to reject the Deity in whom one trusted – this is the wife's stance; the other is to keep clinging to God even in the face of pain and death – this is Job's way.

Job's respect for God may be compared to that of Abraham who was ready to sacrifice his son Isaac, his only son whom he loved and his only hope for the future – to offer the boy as a holocaust. We are not told of the emotions that filled the heart of Abraham as he set out on the journey to obey the terrible divine command, but we do know Job's deep feelings of sorrow. He was not a heartless man. His mourning for his children is expressed in the rending of his clothes and the ancient ritual of shaving his head (1:20), and in the touching words in which he sees no future for himself now except the grave (1:21). Everything worthwhile in life has now been taken from Job with the destruction of his property and his entire family. He feels as naked as the child coming from the mother's womb. He feels that he is now going back empty-handed to the grave, the womb of Mother Earth, so to speak, the earth from which mankind had its origin (Gen 2:9) and to which all must return. In spite of all this he does not turn his back on God, nor does he accuse God of wrongdoing (1:22).

But there was still a further blow to descend on him, afflicting his own person with the gravest illness. He is now severely weakened physically as well as mentally, and it is at this stage that his wife seems to rebuke him for his loyalty to God, and entices him to curse God and die (2:9). His wife thus would have presented the final temptation to Job, and we know how the Church Fathers castigated her as the Devil's Helper (*adjutrix diaboli*, Augustine), and Aquinas' harsh verdict that Satan spared Job's wife so that she could tempt her husband to sin, just as the same Satan brought down the first man by means of a woman. Here we have, in the clearest terms, the linking up of two different stories: the Fall of man (in Gen 3) and the temptation of Job by his wife (Job 2). This conjunction was to have disastrous effects in patristic exegesis, and Aquinas (1226-1274) found it already well established in his sources, his principal one, as far as the Book of Job is concerned, being the massive commentary by Pope Gregory the Great completed during his very difficult pontificate (590-604). Gregory, in his turn, drew on St Augustine (354-430) whom he greatly admired, and whose pet phrase *adjutrix diaboli* Gregory often borrows. None of these three, incidentally, could read a line of Hebrew, the language in which Job was written, and in this respect we might contrast their exegesis with that of Moses Maimonides, the great Jewish scholar (1135-1204), whose brief commentary on Job was compressed into a few pages of his Guide for the Perplexed – on which more later.

When we read Aquinas on Job's wife, then, we are looking at a chain going back through many of the Church Fathers, a *Catena Diabolica*, one might say, in which Job's wife is unfairly linked to the devil, thereby adding to the anti-feminism in medieval spirituality. This is a vast subject beyond my present purposes. What I propose now is to take just one example of a most influential christian writer, Gregory the Great, and his exegesis of the one verse in the Bible spoken by the wife of Job. When Gregory, in *Moralia in Job*, comes to 2:9, he quotes that verse in the Latin translation: 'Benedic Deo', (which, interestingly enough means 'Bless God', not 'curse God', but already exegesis had viewed this 'bless' as a euphemism for 'curse', and so does Gregory) and continues:

'The ancient enemy tempts the human race in two ways, he either breaks those who are firm in heart by tribulations or he weakens them by persecution. He did both in regard to blessed Job. Firstly he inflicted on the father of the family the loss of property, then he devastated the father by the death of his children, and struck him with ulcerous wounds. But in spite of all these blows, Satan saw that Job was holding out, as it were, in the well fortified citadel of virtue. And so Satan took possession of the heart of the wife, as the ladder by which he ascended to the heart of her husband. But all to no avail. He (Job) did not attend to her proposal and taught her the correct way which she accepted. (And now comes an anti-feminist bit; quoting Paul (1 Tim 2:23): 'I do not permit the woman to teach' – she sometimes departs from *wisdom*.)

'The adversary who sees himself repelled from the hearts of good people seeks out those we really love and speaks through their soft words. The power of love penetrates the heart and breaks into the fortification of righteousness. Thus the ancient enemy moved the wife's tongue. Satan spared the woman so that she should tempt her husband.

'Job the holy man was now without any external goods, but within himself he was filled with God's presence, and from within him the treasure of wisdom was born when he replied to his wife in the words of holy learning: 'If we accept good things from the hand of God why should we not put up (*sustineamus*) with evil?'

'The good things are both temporal and eternal; the evil things are the present blows, (quoting Is 45:6,7). It is a great consolation, if we are suffering adversity, to call to mind the good gifts we have already received.

'When Job tells his wife that she has spoken as one of the foolish women (*ex insipientibus mulieribus*) he is finding fault with her sentiments (*sensus*) not with her femininity (*sexus*): (a delightful assonance: '*sensus* … non autem *sexus* in vitio est'). No way does Job say to her, 'you are speaking like a woman', but 'like one of the impious women', to indicate that her fault was not in her being a woman but in taking up an unwise attitude.

'But the Satan went further: he also used Job's three friends to wound Job, thus adding to his temptations.'

Aquinas also considers that the three friends were part of Satan's temptation of Job.

Thus, Gregory, playing on the resemblance between the words *sensus* and *sexus*, and asserting that it's not just Job's wife but also his friends who have become the devil's instruments, has avoided anti-feminist bias to some extent.

There are two serious flaws in Gregory's exegesis of Job 2:9, even though they did not originate with him.

1. The Satan of Job is identified by Gregory with the devil of later theology. But the Satan in Job is not hostile to God, he is simply the Adversary or prosecuting attorney who tests the character of human beings. He holds friendly dialogue with the deity and operates with the latter's permission. He is not the wicked enemy of the Almighty who seeks to drag mankind down into eternal damnation.

In much patristic exegesis, however, the Adversary in Job becomes the outright enemy of God and man. So, when Augustine and Gregory and others called Job's wife the 'Devil's Helper' they blackened her character considerably – and made her a very dangerous woman.

2. The text of Genesis 3 on the temptation and fall of the man through his wife becomes closely linked to the story of Job's wife inciting him to 'curse' God. In both stories there is a triad: the man, the woman, and the serpent/satan. Just as Eve was tempted by the serpent to disobey God, so, the Fathers thought, was Job's wife,

unknown to herself, subtly incited by Satan, to make her husband curse God. One must object immediately at this assumption, which finds no basis in the text of Job. Job's wife had first-hand experience of all her husband's piety over the years and also of all the sorrows the Lord had now inflicted on him. She was like Hannah, the wife of Tobit, the pious and wealthy Israelite who, in spite of all his good deeds, became blind when bird droppings fell into his eyes. Hannah then had to go out and earn money to keep herself and her husband. One day when she returned home with the gift of a young goat, Tobit was convinced she had stolen it and ordered her to return it, whereupon she lost her patience with him and mocked his piety: 'Where are your acts of charity? Where are your righteous deeds?' (Tob 2:14). And, like Job, after being rebuked by his wife, Tobit prays for death to put an end to his anguish (Tob 3). But the point I'm making is that both Hannah and Job's wife had seen with their own eyes the suffering and the humiliation of their husbands, and had shared this sorrow as good wives. They needed no outside incitement from the devil or anyone else to say what they said. (The Book of Tobit was written in Aramaic or Hebrew probably in the third century before Christ; it is preserved in the Greek Old Testament, and is recognised as sacred scripture in the Roman Catholic Canon, but not in the Hebrew Bible).

Likewise, the Greek translator of the Book of Job did not demonise the wife of Job but allowed her to speak with her own voice in the lengthy expansion of 2:9 in the Septuagint. In this expansion the wife fills in several details not found in the Masoretic text. Some of these details concern Job, others concern the wife herself. Concerning Job, she lets us know that throughout his sorrows he still nurtured a hope of his recovery, hoping against hope that his illness was not terminal. Secondly, that he is sitting outside the city on a dungheap (not just 'sitting in ashes', as in the Hebrew). This addition indicates Job's total alienation from society and his consequent humiliation. To add the final sorrow: Job's sores now produce a 'putrefaction of worms'.

Turning to the wife's sorrows, the Septuagint shows that her outburst came only when a long period of time had elapsed after all the calamities had fallen on Job and herself. She had plenty time to consider her words; they were *her* words, from her heart. Also she has been reduced to wandering about looking for menial domestic service to keep bread on the table for Job and herself. A later variant on this theme is found in the pseudepigraphical Testament of Job (written in Greek about 50BC) in which Satan disguises himself as a breadseller and tricks her into letting him cut off her hair in public in exchange for his bread. The Hebrew text of Job, however, nowhere supports this theme of extreme poverty. Job never includes hunger among his many ailments and surely his many relatives listed in chapter 19 would afford him the necessities of life even if they withheld their pity.

In the Septuagint the wife mentions her own special maternal sorrows – in bringing ten children into the world. She has even greater sorrow than Job. Finally, her command to Job, which many have translated as 'Curse God' is softened by the LXX into: *eipon ti rhema eis Kurion*: which could be translated as: 'say something unto (or against) the Lord.'

This tendency of the LXX to soften the harsh language of the Hebrew has been noted by scholars who also point to the LXX's explicit hope of resurrection as part of Job's faith.

The Jewish world of the Diaspora which produced the Septuagint thus felt the need to say something in support of Job's wife, and may well have been drawing on older Hebrew traditions – folk tales as well as written materials – on the Joban themes which the Masoretic text did not reflect. They felt that one single sentence on the wife of Job left too much unsaid: a woman, who suffered as intensely as she, deserved more sympathy than the Masoretes had for her.

If we look over the LXX 'expansion' of 2:9, and join together the first and the last sentences of that passage, we get a syntactical structure identical with the Hebrew but with a difference in theme.

In the LXX, his wife asks Job: 'How long will you hold out, saying look, I will wait a little longer expecting and hoping for my deliverance?' (i.e. from my illness) (2:9a). But say something unto (or against) the Lord and die' (2:9d).

In LXX she is saying that his hoping for a recovery from illness has been going on for far too long a time and that he must acknowledge his death is near and so say something to God before he dies. The 'patience' theme of the LXX is further enhanced in Job's reply which, in the LXX, uses the verb *hypopherein* ('to endure') rather than the Hebrew 'to accept'.

The wife of Job in the LXX is a different woman from that in the MT. In the LXX she speaks as a woman with real feeling for her husband's plight; in the MT (as usually translated) she speaks with the voice and the words of Satan, repeating his 'Curse God' and using the divine eulogy of Job ('retain your integrity') only to mock her husband. Small wonder that so many Church Fathers demonised the woman.

Her advice to Job, in the LXX, may well mean that he should recognise that he now has no hope of recovery and pray to God to put an end to his misery: 'Say some word towards God and die'. Such a prayer Job does actually make later on; in 6:9,10: '... that God would decide to crush me, to let loose his hand and cut me off. Then I should still have the consolation that I had not denied the ordinances of the Holy One.'

Job never contemplates suicide, and his wife never suggests it. The request of a pious man that God would put an end to his life of misery is canonised in the prophet Jeremiah, who like Job curses the day of his birth (Jer 20:14-18), and wishes God had killed him in the womb (20:17). A more explicit prayer for death is found on the lips of the austere prophet Elijah at a time of national apostasy in the Northern Kingdom of Israel, when queen Jezabel persecuted Elijah and he fled south to the wilderness near Beersheba. There he lay down exhausted and depressed and asked God that he might die saying: 'Enough is enough. Now, O Lord, take away my life' (1 Kgs 19:4).

The Lord, however, did not grant his request, nor that of Jonah (Jon 4:1-3) nor that of Job. But the prayer for death as an escape from great misery was not regarded as sinful. And if Job's wife urged him to die, this, of itself, is not an unworthy or cruel sentiment on her part, when one considers all the circumstances.

In the LXX, then, the wife of Job is commenting on her husband's *patient* attitude and asks 'how long more can you hold out', hoping for deliverance from his illness. She feels he has endured enough of pain, and that he should address God directly about his misery and hope to die. Job's reply in the LXX is very touching:

> 2:10 'But he looked on her and said to her you have spoken like one of the foolish women. 2:11 If *we have received* good things from the hand of God, *shall we not endure* (hypoisomen) evil?'

The LXX differs from the Hebrew in introducing the verb 'to endure': Job's patient endurance is not yet exhausted – that will come later (6:8-10), and Job feels that true wisdom calls for endurance rather than escape from sorrows through death. His wife's view, according to Job, is contrary to religious wisdom and so he uses the term 'foolish' as the opposite of wise. But, of course, he doesn't say she's foolish, but that she has just spoken *like* a foolish woman. And he invites her to share his endurance: 'shall we not endure', just as she shared his prosperity in the past: the LXX uses the aorist and the future tenses to distinguish the two different periods of their fortunes.

Job's reply, in the LXX, confirms this emphasis on patience (rather than integrity) as the topic of his wife's statement.

Job, in the LXX, uses the verb *hypopherein* – to endure, the operative function of patience, and he uses the first person plural of the verb, saying to her 'shall *we* not endure evil?'. In his use of 'we' he acknowledges the sufferings of his wife; she and he are partners in sorrow. The LXX furthermore touchingly notes that while saying this 'he looked on her'. Job is now speaking as a husband to the wife he loves, and he wishes she would share his own deeply religious attitude ('wisdom') in the face of the ultimate crises of their life together: to endure the evil the Lord had sent on them rather than try to escape from it into the tranquillity of death: this would be 'foolish' (not intellectual stupidity, but religious weakness).

Before we finally leave the Hebrew text of 2:9 with its seemingly dreadful portrait of Job's wife, perhaps we could seek one faint ray of redemptive hope for her in the verb she uses: *Barekh*, which many have been translating as 'Curse' but which properly means 'Bless'. Job himself was the last to use this verb when he accepted God's will with the words: 'May the name of the Lord be blessed' (1:21). If then we take the benign view of the wife's statement, she would be simply urging her husband to persevere in his integrity, to bless God and face death. Job's rebuke would then centre on the final advice, 'face death'; he wishes to endure rather than escape.

Her statement could be taken *not* necessarily as a question: 'Do you still maintain your integrity?' but, in view of the absence of the interrogative particle in the Hebrew, as a statement of fact: 'You are still holding fast to your integrity, bless God and die'. The idea being that it would be better for her husband to die blessing God than to break down under his ongoing sufferings and turn away from God. (It is curious that Aquinas, in his exposition on Job, considers the possibility that the wife's 'bless' means just that, and not 'curse' as most commentators would say. We have to realise that the author of the Prologue is a very subtle sage who, throughout his naïve story, has interwoven hints of theological enigma.)

Job's response to this would be that the proper (or 'wise') thing for him and for her was to go on enduring the sorrows the Lord sent them ('we sustain'), and that to look for death would be 'foolish' from a religious point of view. It would be like Jonah's angry prayer for death (Jonah 4:3) for which the Lord rebuked him.

Thus we may consider that the wife, in calling on her husband to bless God, really wishes him to continue in his religious attitude which he himself already expressed in his famous 'May the name of the Lord be blessed' (1:21). This is an unusual formula which seems to call on other people (especially his wife who was the only one to hear his original prayer) to bless God's name also. This formula also occurs in Psalm 113:2 where others ('the servants of the Lord', 113:1) are asked to join in the psalmists' praise for the Lord who 'raises the poor from the *ashes*' (113:7), the same word as in Job 2:8.

The wife's words could then be considered as in tune with the blessing motif. She is happy that he 'still' holds fast to his piety. The word 'still' on her lips (in 2:9) denotes a greater burden of suffering than it did in 2:3 when Job had not yet been stricken with his illness. She knows that her husband's piety is being stretched to the limit so she wishes him to bless God once more and then look for death as a release, perhaps by praying for it as Elijah did in his distress. But Job wants to endure whatever the Lord sends. His rejection of his wife's advice concerns, I suggest, only this one matter of dying, and is the only sentiment in which he disagrees with her. Her remark Job finds unworthy of her, a woman whom he always regarded as a superior lady, far above the ordinary women of the locality. He sees her advice as a temporary lapse, completely out of character. For this reason he seeks to draw her closer to his ways of thinking by using the first person plural: 'we' (you and I) have seen good times together all our lifetime up to recently, should we now not accept the bad things that have begun to afflict us?

This all-embracing piety of Job, accepting the good and the bad, and praising God for both is, I suppose, difficult for modern readers to accept and we are left with the impression that Job has gone too far, lost his sanity, in being too uncritical of the Lord's hard ways.

Yet this all-embracing attitude was not regarded in Jewish piety as being required only by exceptionally saintly figures. We, today, are not made of such strong piety. We bless God for his goodness to us, but we rarely think of blessing him for our illnesses, early deaths of our children, destruction of our homes.

In the Jewish book called the *Mishnah* we find that what Job did is what every man should do: 'Man is bound to bless God for the evil as he blesses God for the good. Thou shalt love the Lord thy God ... with all thy soul, even if he (God) takes away thy soul ...' (*Berakoth*, 9:5, abbreviated). The result is that if a man prays thanking God 'for the good', he is silenced (Ber 3:5). A man must praise God for both the good and the evil. Job observed this piety when in 1:21 he prayed 'May God's name be blessed' immediately after his confession that the Lord had both 'given' and 'taken'.

Job's wife had been witness to this prayer. She had also been witness both to the divine giving and taking, and now heard her husband's wish that she should join in blessing the name of the Lord. Her husband didn't say 'Blessed be the name of the Lord', using the usual form *Barukh* (past participle *Qal* of the verb *Brk*) which would reflect Job's own praise and adoration for God. He used a different form (the *Piel*, or intensive form of the verb) which was used in the liturgy calling on other believers present to bless God: 'May the name of the Lord be blessed' (by those present). Since his wife may be presumed to have been with Job when he uttered this prayer, it was an invitation to her to enter into his sentiments of blessing, of praise and adoration of God, as in Psalm 113:2, already quoted.

When, then, she later says to Job 'Bless God' she is, let us suppose, *not* using the verb 'bless' as a euphemism for 'curse', as most commentators have thought, but in its original sense of praising God, as her husband did.

The Hebrew verb *Brk* in the *Piel* (or intensive) form is used only on the rarest occasions as a euphemism for 'curse'; its normal meaning is *bless*, and Hebrew had perfectly normal words for curse when it wished to use them. When the Hebrew Bible uses *Brk* as a euphemism it relies on the intelligence of the reader (or listener) to understand this from the context. Thus when Job offered sacrifices for his children in case 'they sinned and blessed God in their hearts' (1:5) the context clearly requires 'blessed' to be understood as 'cursed', and when Satan says that if God withdraws Job's prosperity Job 'will bless you (God) to your face' (1:11;2:5) the 'bless' stands for 'curse'.

In the cases just cited, the context leaves us in no doubt that *Brk* stands for 'curse'. But now we come to the famous statement by Job's wife in which she says to Job: 'Bless (*Brk*) God' (2:9). Does the context here clearly require us to interpret her as saying 'curse God'? If we are reading the Book of Job in a modern translation, most translators decide the question for us in advance: they translate the verb *Brk* as 'curse'. This, however, deprives the reader of entry into the enigma and the ambiguity in which the Hebrew author wanted to involve him. The author of Job was a subtle sage who wanted to get the reader involved in the search for meaning, the meaning of life and of language, and the meaning, so full of anguish, in the heart of a woman whose life has been ruined.

In contrast to many modern translations, early versions of Job 2:9 studiously avoided putting the words 'Curse God' on the lips of Job's wife. Thus the Aramaic translation, the Targum on Job, while it has no hesitation with Satan's hope that Job would eventually *curse* God (using the verb 'curse' and not the euphemistic 'bless', in 1:11 and 2:5) retains the verb 'to bless' for the wife's statement (2:9), thus presenting her in a more favourable light.

The Septuagint version also avoids the crude blasphemy of 'Curse God' on the wife's lips (in 2:9) by giving us the ambiguous 'say something *eis* (Greek: *unto* or possibly *against*) God'.

It is interesting to observe how St John Chrysostom (c.347-407), who commented on the Septuagint version of Job, approached 2:9. He sees it as the wife's adverse criticism of God's harsh ways but explicitly denies it amounted to blasphemy. Chrysostom, perhaps the greatest stylist among the Greek Fathers, had, during his turbulent years as patriarch of Constantinople, learned much about feminine psychology, not least from his unhappy conflict with the empress Eudoxia. He comments on the Septuagintal text which expands considerably on Job's wife and on what she says to Job concerning her own pain at the loss of her children, and the hardships she has been enduring now for a long time trying to feed her destitute husband. It is out of all this pain that she eventually speaks, says Chrysostom. He stresses that Job, while rejecting her irreverent sentiments, did not reject his wife, but tried to win her over to his own pious acceptance of God's will. He does not call his wife stupid; she is a well-educated lady but her remark was unworthy of her. He tells her that the sorrows they now both endure were not because of any sinfulness on their part, just as their former prosperity was not a reward for their piety.

Let us turn now to the Latin Fathers, to St Jerome (347-420), the most learned biblical translator of his time. In his famous translation of the Bible into Latin, known as the Vulgate, he was well aware of the differences between the Hebrew, Greek, and Old Latin texts of Job. He was a strong proponent of the primacy of the Hebrew text, and accordingly when he came to translate Job 2:9 he loyally followed the Hebrew in which Job's wife says 'Bless (*Brk*) God', and so he gave us 'Benedic Deo', even though in his exegetical writing he castigates her and regards her words as a euphemism for 'curse God'. Jerome could be very crude and offensive to married women, as is clear in his famous Letter to Eustochium, the sixteen-year-old Roman girl, who was studying the Hebrew bible under his tutorship, and whom he encouraged to a life of virginity by listing the disadvantages of marriage. But he was too good a translator to impose his exegesis or his prejudice on the text of the Vulgate, and he allows the reader to use his/her own intelligence, just as the Hebrew text did.

When Aquinas, in his large commentary (*Expositio*) on Job, came to 2:9, he quotes the Latin text: *Benedic Deo* (Bless God) and goes on to give two interpretations of it. The first follows what had then become the traditional patristic line that she really meant 'Curse God' and thus was helping the devil to destroy her husband's piety. The second interpretation, however, is fascinating and deserves an airing too. In it he takes the opposite view, viz. that she really meant what she said: her 'Bless God' means just that. Aquinas writes:

> Her words 'bless God and die' may also be understood as saying: seeing that your great reverence for God has brought such tragic consequences on you, if you persist in blessing God you can only expect to die.
> (*Vel aliter, Benedic Deo et morere, id est ex quo tantam reverentiam sic adversitate afflictus es, si adhuc Deo benedicas nihil restat nisi ut mortem expectes.*)

If Jerome had followed the manner of many modern translators and written *Maledic* ('curse') in 2:9, Aquinas would probably never have given us the little gem just quoted. Most English readers of Job have the good name of Job's wife blackened for them from the beginning when they hear her saying 'Curse God and die'. Much better if they first read what she actually is reported to have said: 'Bless God', and then let them make up their own minds if she meant the opposite or not.

But to return to Aquinas' second ('benign') view of Job's wife. For a man whose life was hedged around with monastic celibacy from his tenderest years (in Benedictine and Dominican seclusion) he shows an extra-ordinary openness to the genre of conjugal dialogue.

Job and his wife are not holding a public debate on theodicy. They are talking in the briefest colloquy on the sudden collapse of their affluent world. When Michal reproached her husband David, it was also brief and to the point; but it was wounding because she already despised her husband in her heart (2 Sam:6:16-23). There is nothing to suggest such venom in the wife of Job. She is more like the kind-hearted Hannah reproaching her blinded husband Tobit for all his futile prayers. She loves her husband, and her words are not meant to hurt but to enlighten him. Similarly, in Aquinas' 'benign' interpretation she genuinely feels that Job's life-long practice of offering of sacrifices to God for his children really did them harm, not good, and that he'll only bring final disaster on himself by continuing in his piety. Job's reply to her then (2:10) would mean not that she was blaspheming, but that she was speaking like the silly women down the town and that both he and she had received many good things from God in the past, and must now put up with the evil side of life. In Job 2:9,10 we are listening in to a private and frank conversation between a wife and a husband who still love one another and are trying to unfathom the terrible tragedy that has engulfed their lives. Intriguing as this view is, Aquinas leaves it without further exploration, and continues his exegesis drawing on Gregory's *Moralia*, and in a more lucid Latinity compressing into one relative clause all the worst things you could say about the wife of Job: 'whom alone the devil spared so that through her he who had defeated the first man by means of a woman might assail the mind of a just man.' (*quam solam diabolus reliquerat ut per eam viri justi mentem pulsaret qui per feminam primum hominem pulsaret*). Aquinas, *Expositio super Job, in loco.*

Aquinas composed his *Expositio* on Job while teaching in Paris 1269-1272. He was at the height of his intellectual powers, and only a few years before his early death (1274). He had already compiled the massive *Catena Aurea*, the Golden Chain of patristic exegesis of the four gospels, in which he, Aquinas, showed how varied and even contradictory views of gospel texts had been held by the great Christian thinkers of the past. In his work on Job, while he follows the main line of earlier commentators in their harsh treatment of Job's wife, feeling, no doubt, that in his public lectures to students, he was expected to pay homage to the traditions of the past, he nevertheless was bold enough to indicate that there was a more benign wife of Job than the one generally portrayed.

The whole weight of exegetical tradition (and not just St Augustine) weighs against this unfortunate lady and regards her as inciting her husband to blaspheme God. One reason for this is, I suppose, that Job uses the term 'foolish' to describe her sentiments, a term which can mean 'blasphemous', and so would fittingly describe her if she really had said to Job 'Curse God'. But the word 'foolish' can also be understood as merely 'silly', 'ignoble', 'vulgar'. Now Job, if the truth be told, was quite a snob, in spite of his piety. He was proud of his high position in society and enjoyed the deference of the lower classes 'whose fathers I would have distained to put with the dogs who kept my flocks' (30:1).

Job feels that his wife, by urging him to seek release from his ongoing illness through death, is voicing the sentiments of low-class women. If 'thoroughbreds don't cry' applies to Job, it should apply to his wife also, he thinks. He intends to accept his sorrows, not escape from them, and he would hope for her support in this.

Later on, as his illness continues, he will pray for death as a release from his woes (6:9-10; 7:15,16). But just now he intends to carry his burden.

If Job, in 1:21, could invite his wife (and others) to join with him in praising the God who had both given and taken away, (See David J.A. Clines, *Job 1-20*, Dallas, Texas, 1989, p 39. See also *Mishnah, Berakoth* 9,3: 'A man should say the Benediction for misfortune regardless of good, and for good fortune regardless of evil') she, in her turn, could express her total devotion to God by using the invitatory form of the Blessing Psalms (66:8; 92:2; 100:4; 103:1; 104:1; 134:1,2; 135:19; 145:10,21 – all of which use the Piel Imperative, as in Job 2:9), blessing God even in the face of death: such an act of prayer *in extremis* is also reflected in the *Misnah* passage already quoted: 'You shall love the Lord your God with all your soul, even if he takes your soul away' (Berakoth 9:5). Thus both Job (1:21) and his wife (2:9) may have been using the prayerful language of the Psalms of Blessing in their holy colloquy.

Death by stoning is the punishment laid down in Leviticus 24:10-16 for blasphemy. Two conditions are required before the offence can be committed, viz. one must speak contemptuously of God, and also utter the sacred name *Yhwh* (usually translated 'the Lord').

Some questions: If Job had cursed God, who would have stoned him to death? Would his wife have to give evidence at his trial? And if she really did mean 'Curse God' when she spoke, wouldn't she have been guilty of blasphemy by incitement?

And if Job understood his wife as urging him to curse God, would he not have felt obliged to have sacrifices offered as expiation for her sin, as he had done for his own children earlier (1:6)?

All these questions are rarely addressed by exegetes who translate 2:9 as 'Curse God and die'.

When you are reading the Book of Job for the first time and you come to the wife's laconic 'die' (2:9), she seems a heartless woman with no warmth, no comforting words for her husband. But when you are reading Job for the second or third time (and a great book deserves a second read) you begin to see her in a softer light, and to appreciate her admiration for her husband's continuing piety, her prayerful invitation to him to bless (praise) God even in adversity, and her realistic evaluation of his spiritual limits. She was anticipating the decline in spiritual energy which her husband was to admit to later on: in chapter 3 with his *wish* for death, and in chapters 6 and 7 with his *prayer* for death. She felt that the exalted spirituality of his early utterances (1:21) would not last indefinitely, and she was right in this.

In fairness to the Church Fathers, however, it must be stated that the process which ended in the joining of Gen 3 and Job 2 had already started some hundreds of years before the Christian era. In the Wisdom of Solomon (which formed part of the Septuagint), we find the earliest known identification of the serpent of Gen 3 with the devil: 'But by the devil's envy death entered the world' (2:24). Then the serpent/devil/Satan are rolled into one evil spiritual being, for ever inciting mankind to turn away from God. And it was the Septuagint version, rather than the shorter Hebrew Bible (which didn't contain the Wisdom of Solomon) that became the Bible of the early Christian church, and of the Fathers.

As a result of this fusion, the phrase 'The Devil's Helper' became a lot more sinister than it would be if the Satan of the Job story (Job 1 & 2) were taken in its original meaning, viz. the Adversary at the heavenly court who acts only with divine permission and is forbidden to take the life of Job. It is true that *if* she urged her husband to 'curse God' she is helping the Adversary's cause, and so, technically, she is the Adversary's Helper even if she is not aware of this, but this Adversary is not the enemy of God seeking man's eternal death. He's only a 'little devil', so to speak.

But to return to Gregory: When he draws on his own insights and gives us such a pleasing assonance as 'sensus ... non sexus in vitio est' he shows no anti-feminism. Gregory's experience of life at the highest level of civil administration – he was prefect of the city of Rome in 572 at the age of 32 – allowed him contact with men and women in all walks of life. His great grandfather had been the saintly Pope Felix III (Pope 483-492) whose wife died while he was still a deacon, and who was pleased to call her 'Levitae conjux' on her tombstone. Gregory himself became a deacon and, after relinquishing his civil post, became papal nuncio in Constantinople. The most fascinating page in his commentary on Job from the feminist point of view is his praise of the women disciples of Jesus for their greater fidelity to Jesus than all the apostles put together.

He bases himself on the text of Mark 14:50 that when Jesus was captured in the Garden of Gethsemane on the eve of his death, all the male disciples fled. The holy women, on the contrary, not only did not run away, they were not afraid, and they stayed with Jesus right to Calvary and to the tomb. They gave to Jesus the loyalty his male disciples were expected to give but failed. All this, incidentally, forms the bulk of his comment on Job 19:20, 'My bones cling to my

skin, my flesh having been consumed', where he takes 'bones' to
refer to Christ, 'flesh' to the disciples who were consumed with
fear, and fled, and 'skin' to the holy women who clung to Christ
throughout. As can be seen, Gregory can stretch the meaning of a
text to surprising lengths. See Gregory's *Moralium* Lib. XIV, in
Caput *XIX Job* (Migne, P.L., LXXV, 1068).

Job's wife and anti-feminism
If Job's use of the 'domestic *we*' is accepted, it shows his consciousness of his wife as his partner in life. But the author of the Book of
Job is writing for a man's world, in which a woman has no independent personality. He doesn't even tell us her name or her family
background, he doesn't indicate if she comforted her husband in
his ongoing illness. It allows no time for her to mourn her own
children, as Rachel mourned hers; it doesn't mention her ever again
after the fleeting reference to her in 19:17 when she is nauseated by
Job's halitosis. And when Job's second family arrives at the very end,
we are not sure who the mother is. All these matters are addressed in
later Jewish literature, but this is not our present concern.

The patient Job of the Prologue can speak gently to his wife,
using the language of conjugal partnership, the 'domestic *we*', as
Murial Spark so well puts it in her Joban novel, *The Only Problem*.
But the impatient Job of the Dialogue has no tender words for his
long-suffering wife who is still with him (19:17). His most cruel
remark about her comes in his self-imprecation that if he had been
guilty of adultery his wife should suffer humiliation in two ways:

> If my heart had been enticed by a woman,
> If I lurked at my neighbour's door,
> Let my wife grind for another,
> And others bend over her (31:9,10).

For a man to pray that, as a punishment for his own adultery, his
wife, the innocent party, should be violated by another man is
unique in the literature of shame. The 'grind' may refer to her being
the slave of another, but the final line is far more evil.

As if aware of the unfair treatment allotted to women in his
work, the author (or editor) gives us the names of Job's three beautiful daughters with the added bonus that their father made generous provision for them, giving them an equal share in the inheritance with their brothers, something unheard of in Jewish Law
(42:14,15). Too little too late, one might say.

Who can remember the names of the three daughters? But who
can forget the wife of Job?

Summary: The wife of Job
(In Chapters 1-3)

In the whole length of the Book of Job there is only one sentence devoted to the wife of Job. In it (2:9) she issues three strong challenges to her husband: firstly, she asks him why, in view of all the calamities God has inflicted on him, he continues in his piety; secondly, she urges him to 'Bless God', which most commentators take to be a euphemism for 'Curse' God – surely a dreadful word to speak to a devout man – and thirdly – and very strangely for a wife – she commands her husband to die.

Her one, never to be forgotten, sentence stands exactly midway in the three opening chapters of Job. There are 30 verses before it, and 30 after it. The sentiments expressed in it relate both to what went before and what came after she uttered it.

When she says 'You still hold fast to your piety', that little word 'still' shows she has been close to her husband in all the bitter experiences recounted so far: the loss of their property, of all their ten children, and finally Job's own painful and humiliating illness.

But her words not only reflect the past events, they also determine the responses of Job in what follows.

Job responds (2:10), rejecting her sentiments but trying to win her over to his own total acceptance of God's will, even when it brings evil to both of them. Later, however, Job will be haunted by her dark word 'Die'. Job *wishes* for death (chap 3), and *prays* for death (chap 6). His three friends arrive to comfort him (2:11-13). They are so appalled at his sufferings that they remain silent, sitting with him for seven days.

Job breaks the silence and responds in one of the great poems of lamentation in all the Bible. All of chapter three (verse 1-26) is Job's death-wish; it is a soliloquy, not addressed to God, nor to the friends, nor even to his wife. Job is now speaking the language of death, and in this he is responding positively to the sentiments expressed so forcefully by his wife. He agrees with her in wishing for death as a welcome release from life's anguish.

By a curious irony, Job's friend Eliphaz will soon (chap 4)

reproach Job for his death-wish, in much the same way as Job himself had reproached his wife for suggesting it (2:9,10). Eliphaz in chapter 4 is not suggesting that Job's wish to die is blasphemous, but he still regards it as a serious failure in a person of such exalted virtue as Job. This fact surely suggests that his wife's advice to Job to die was also not blasphemous, but simply unworthy of her and that this is what Job's reproach to her (2:10) amounts to.

At first Job thought he could bear all his sorrows with patience (2:10), but after months of pain (7:3) he cannot suppress his anguish. But while he recognises God as the cause of his distress, he does not accuse God of injustice (as he will do later) but asks for death while he still respects God (6:9,10).

The Wife of Job
Chapters 1-3

The piety and wealth of Job 1:1-5
1 There was once a man in the land of Uz, whose name was Job, and
that man was blameless and upright, and he feared God and avoided
evil. 2 And there were born to him seven sons and three daughters;
3 and his possessions were seven thousand yoke of oxen, and five
hundred she-asses, and a very great household. And that man was
the greatest of all the people of the east. 4 Now his sons used to go
and hold a feast in the house of each in turn, and to send and invite
their three sisters to eat and drink with them. 5 And when the days
of their feasting were over. Job used to sanctify them; and he arose
early in the morning and offered holocausts according to the number of them all. For Job said: 'It may be that my children have sinned,
and blessed God in their hearts.' So did Job always.

The first dialogue in heaven 1:6-12
6 Now the day came when the sons of God came to present themselves before the Lord, and Satan also came in the midst of them. 7
And the Lord said to Satan: 'Where did you come from?' And Satan
answered the Lord and said: 'From roaming the earth, and walking
to and fro therein.' 8 And the Lord said to Satan: 'Have you noticed
my servant Job? There is none like him on the earth, a man blameless and upright, who fears God and avoids evil.' 9 And Satan
answered the Lord and said: 'Is it without reason that Job fears
God? 10 Have you not made a hedge about him and his house, and
about all that is his on every side? The work of his hands you have
blessed, and his possessions have increased in the land; 11 but put
forth your hand, and touch all that he has, surely, he will bless you
to your face.' 12 And the Lord said to Satan: 'Behold, all that he has
is in your power, only against himself put not forth your hand.'
And Satan went forth from the presence of the Lord.

The first calamities: Property and children 1:13-22
13 And the day came when his sons and his daughters were drink-

ing wine in the house of their eldest brother, 14 and a messenger
came to Job, and said: 'The oxen were ploughing, and the she-asses
grazing near them, 15 and the Sabeans made a raid and took them,
and the servants they smote with the edge of the sword, and I only
have escaped, alone to tell you.'

17 And while he was still speaking, another came and said:
'Chaldeans made themselves into three bands, and fell upon the
camels and took them, and the servants they smote with the edge of
the sword, and I only have escaped, alone to tell you.' 18 And while
he was still speaking, another came and said: 'Your sons and
daughters were eating and drinking in the house of their eldest
brother, 19 and behold, a great wind came from beyond the wilderness, and smote the four corners of the house, and it fell upon the
young people and they died, and I only have escaped, alone to tell
you.' 20 And Job arose, and rent his mantle, and shaved his head,
and fell to the ground and bowed himself, and said: 21 'Naked I
came forth from my mother's womb, and naked shall I return; the
Lord gave, and the Lord has taken away; blessed be the name of the
Lord!' 22 In all this Job did not sin or charge God with unseemli-
ness.

The second dialogue in heaven 2:1-6
2:1 And the day came when the sons of God came to present themselves before the Lord, and Satan also came in the midst of them to
present himself before the Lord. 2 And the Lord said to Satan:
'Where did you come from?' And Satan answered the Lord and
said: 'From roaming the earth, and walking to and fro therein.' 3
And the Lord said to Satan: 'Have you noticed my servant Job?
There is none like him on the earth, a man blameless and upright,
one that fears God and avoids evil; and he still holds fast to his
integrity, and in vain have you moved me against him to destroy
him.' 4 And Satan answered the Lord and said: 'Skin, for skin, and
all that a man has will he give for his life: 5 but put forth your hand,
and touch his bone and his flesh, surely, he will bless you to your
face.' 6 And the Lord said unto Satan: 'Behold, he is in your power,
only spare his life.'

The second calamity: Job's health in ruins 2:7,8
7 And Satan went forth from the presence of the Lord, and he smote
Job with a grievous ulcer, from the sole of his foot to his crown; 8
and he took him a potsherd to scrape himself with, and he sat
among the ashes.

The wife of Job speaks 2:9
9 And his wife said to him: 'You are still holding fast to your integrity! Bless God and die.'

Job's first response 2:10
10 But he said to her: 'As one of the foolish women might speak, so you speak! Indeed, it is good things we have been receiving from God, and shall we not receive evil?' In all this Job did not sin with his lips.

The silent comforters 2:11-13
11 And when Job's three friends heard of all this misfortune that was come upon him, they came every one from his own place, Eliphaz the Temanite, Bildad the Shuhite, and Sophar the Namaathite; and they met together by appointment, to come to condole with him, and to comfort him. 12 And when they lifted up their eyes afar off, they knew him not; so they cried out and wept, and each rent his mantle, and they threw dust upon their heads in desolation. 13 And they sat down with him upon the ground, seven days and seven nights, and none spoke a word unto him; for they saw that his sorrow was very great.

Job's second response: *a) A curse 3:1-9*
          b) A death wish 3:10-26

a) 1 After this, Job broke the silence and cursed his day.
  2 And Job answered and said:
  3 Perish the day on which I was born,
   And the night which said: 'A boy is conceived.'
  4 That day, let it be darkness!
   Let not God regard it from above,
   Neither let the light shine upon it!
  5 Let darkness and death-shade claim it!
   Let clouds settle upon it!
   Let the day's eclipse affright it!
  6 That night, let dense darkness seize it!
   Let it not be united with the days of the year,
   Into the number of the months let it not come!
  7 Lo, that night, let it be desolate!
   Let no joyous shouting enter it!
  8 Let them curse it that curse the day,
   That are ready to rouse up Leviathan!

9 Let the stars of its twilight be darkened!
    Let it look for light, but look in vain!
    And let it not behold the eyelids of the dawn!

b) 10 Oh would that He had shut up the doors of the womb,
    And so hid trouble from mine eyes!
11 Why did I not die at birth?
    Come forth from the womb and expire?
12 Why did the knees receive me?
    And why the breasts, that I should suck?
13 For then I should have lain down, and been quiet,
    I should have slept, then rest had been mine;
14 With kings and counsellors of the earth,
    Who had restored ruined palaces for themselves;
15 Or with princes who had possessed gold,
    Who had filled their houses with silver;
16 Or like the hidden, still-born babe, that was not,
    Like infants who never saw the light.
17 There the wicked cease from troubling,
    And there the weary are at rest;
18 The prisoners are at ease together,
    And hear not the voice of the taskmaster;
19 Small and great, there are the same,
    And the servant is free from his master.
20 Why is light given to one that is in travail?
    And life to those in sorrow?
21 Who long for death, and it comes not,
    And seek for it more than for hidden treasures;
22 Who are glad unto exultation,
    And rejoice when they reach the grave;
23 To a man whose way is hid,
    And whom God has hedged in?
24 For my sighing is my food,
    And my groans are poured out as water;
25 Should I fear a thing, it comes upon me,
    And that which I dread comes to me;
26 I have no ease, and I have no quiet,
    And I have no rest, and trouble comes.

CHAPTER 2

The comforters

The theme of comforting the afflicted is quite important throughout the whole Book of Job. In the Prologue (2:11) the friends set out to comfort Job; in the Epilogue (42:11) his relatives do likewise. In the poem the verb *nḥm* (in Piel) and its derivatives (6:10) and (15:11; 21:2) is used in the same sense: 'to comfort' (someone). But in the body of the poem Job, always seeking comfort in his sorrows, never finds it. His friends are 'miserable comforters' (16:2). When he hoped 'my bed will comfort me' his hopes were dashed by disturbing dreams (7:13). If his friends would only listen to his words of lament they would afford him some consolation (21:2). He is so oppressed by sorrow that he would find consolation in death (6:10). Eliphaz puts to Job the argument that the consolation of his religion ought to comfort him:

> Are the consolations of God too small for you?
> And the word that treats you gently? (15:11)

a beautiful line stressing God's gentleness towards those who commit some sin: once they repent, God will deliver them from their sufferings. But Job finds their arguments false, and so asks 'How then will you comfort me with empty nothings?' (21:34). He has no sin for which to repent. Job fails all through the poem to find consolation, not indeed that a consoling word 'spoken gently to him' would have removed his physical suffering, but it would have eased his mental anguish somewhat.

Sympathy without words
When Job's three friends Eliphaz, Bildad, and Zophar heard of all his calamities they arranged to come and condole with him and comfort him.

But when they first saw him from a distance they did not recognise him, and they wept aloud, rent their cloaks, and tossed dust into the air.

For seven days and seven nights they sat beside him on the ground, and none of them said a word to him; for they saw that his suffering was very great (2:11-13).

Silent sympathy for the innocent sufferer – a theme rarely touched on in the Bible as explicitly as in the passage just quoted from Job – is a subject of great art in all ages. Of all Edvard Munch's early paintings his 'Sick Child' (1885-1886) stands out as the most important, as representing an inner experience of sympathy for the young girl who is looking hopefully towards the light streaming in the window, while the mother sitting at the bedside bows her head in silent sorrow. The artist worked on this picture for a whole year and drew on his own feelings of desolation (the death of his mother and his sister) to express the tragedy of young suffering.

Turning to poetry, and not merely to the poetry of words, but to the poetry of life, we have a superb moment of sympathy both with words and without words:

> Rose frail and fair – yet frailest
> A wonder wild
> In gentle eyes thou veilest
> My blueveined child.

In James Joyce's poem 'A Flower Given to My Daughter' (Trieste 1913) he speaks not merely from poetic imagination but from the fullness of a father's tenderness for his only daughter Lucia, a girl of rare artistic talent who was afflicted with a progressive mental illness that was to last all her life. When, during the Second World War, Joyce settled in La Baule and visited his daughter daily in the nearby nursing home, he was the only one who hoped for some little improvement in her condition, and his hope was that this would happen 'as a miracle from paternal love'. How did the sick girl perceive her father's presence? To offer consolation and hope to some afflicted soul is one thing; for the afflicted one to experience the consoling presence of a friend is another. Lucia was an artist, and in the drawing of her father's face (in Jane Lidderdale's collection) she gives the answer to our question. Whereas Joyce had his portrait made by several portraitists – Augustus John, Paul-Emile Becat, Adolf Hoffmeister, Otto Christensen, Ivan Opffer and others – his daughter Lucia produced the gentlest of expressions on the face of her father. In her portrait of her father the strong lines of his determined face have melted into the softness of tears. He has poemed her flower-frail mind, and she penetrated the frail inner core of the great man, and perceived the father's perplexity at life's cruel ways. Her portrait shows the bewildered eyes of the father, eyes that suffered from several operations, none really successful, eyes which other artists had politely left blank or showed only at side-face.

Lucia came closer to a full-face of her subject than most and what she showed was that she was consoled by her father's presence – even if she was not cured. Joyce sitting with his afflicted daughter, and the three friends sitting with Job: silence and sympathy.

Words of comforting may be spoken when there is a hope of recovery, but when no such hope exists, when the sorrow seems set to continue indefinitely, this sympathetic silence may be the only balm for the unhealing wound, as Job's three friends saw when they first arrived to visit him in his sorrow, 'to condole with him and comfort him' (2:11); 'And they sat with him on the ground seven days and seven nights, and no one spoke a word to him, for they saw that his grief was very great' (2:13).

Comforting without words, because the grief of Job is so great that even the well-intentioned words of his best friends would only serve to hurt him further. Comforting simply by being present to the sufferer, by lamenting and weeping for him and performing other symbolic gestures of grief (v.12), which our modern Western mentality no longer appreciates.

This passage just quoted (2:11-13) is without parallel in the Bible. It was so highly valued by ancient Jewish sages that they modelled the ritual of mourning (e.g. the rubric that visitors remain silent until the mourner speaks first) partly on this biblical passage. Unfortunately the passage is sometimes underrated by comment-ators who introduce, before its proper time, Job's rejection of the 'cold comfort' of his three friends.

The passage should be appreciated in its present context, and we need be in no doubt that we are being drawn into a work of superior literary art of immense psychological insight.

Sympathy by listening
> 'Listen carefully to my words
> and let this be the consolation you offer me' (21:2).

We are so accustomed to feeling that we have to 'say something' to a sorrowing person that it is only with difficulty we read verses like that just quoted. Yet the ancient art of comforting, so richly doc-umented in book of Job, not only laid down the rubric of 'sympathy without words' (2:9-13) but also 'sympathy by listening', by letting the sufferer speak out his sorrow without correction or interruption from the listener.

> 'A true friend should stand by the sufferer, even if the latter
> forsakes the fear of God' (6:14 – an obscure text).

Job expects his three friends not only to listen to his groaning but also to attend to his criticism of the Almighty concerning the lack of justice in the world. Chapter 21 begins and ends with the theme of 'comforting' almost like an antiphon (21:2,32) and the whole chapter shows that the comfort which Job seeks from his friends is that which they would afford by listening to his 'arguments from experience' of the triumph of the wicked man in the world:

> Have you not asked those who travel the roads, and do you not accept this testimony, that the wicked man is spared in the day of calamity, that he is rescued on the day of wrath? Who declares his way to his face, and who requites him for what he has done? When he is borne to the grave, watch is kept over his tomb, the clods of the valley are sweet to him. All men follow after him, and those who go before him are innumerable. How then will you comfort me with empty nothings? There is nothing left of your answers but falsehood (21:29-34).

'Comforting by listening' is what Job is asking from friends (21:2). This may not seem to us to offer much consolation to an afflicted man. But we may note that, in the passage quoted, Job is not talking about his own personal ailments, but has broadened his perspective to consider the triumphant funeral of the wicked man. Such consolation does not take away the physical pain, but it affords a soothing to the troubled mind of Job that he can reason about his condition, he can seek the truth and express it and hope that a sympathetic ear will listen. The consolation of Wisdom: a wise man is consoled in his sorrow by being able to speak the truth about the human condition.

Comforting by a word of promise (Chapters 4 & 5)
Long before the Consolation of Philosophy was penned by Boethius languishing in prison, and long before the consolatory genre was explored by Cicero, Seneca and others, the prophetic literature bearing the names of Jeremiah, Isaiah, and Ezechiel addressed a word of consolation and of hope to the Jewish exiles suffering in Babylon. What these prophets say to the people as a whole, Eliphaz now says to Job, viz. that after a period of suffering he will once more be restored to health and prosperity by God. This is a word of consolation. 'Does not the consolation of God suffice you, a word that treats you gently?' (15:11).

Eliphaz, in his first speech (chapters 4&5) takes this approach in a truly urbane and sophisticated presentation of the traditional doctrine of divine retribution. Job, says Eliphaz, has led a religious life

and has been blameless before God, and this very fact should now
bring him comfort and hope for an improvement in his condition
because God will never allow a blameless man to perish. Perdition
is only for the wicked. Of course Eliphaz does intimate that Job
must have some fault, but then no man can be totally blameless in
the sight of the Almighty (4:7), all human creatures are fragile, and
are 'born to trouble' (5:17). God does punish people for their faults,
but such a punishment can be a blessing in disguise and can bring
us back to God again; then 'the hand (of God) that smites Job will
also heal him' (5:18).

Eliphaz is careful not to speculate whether any of Job's presumed faults were deliberate or indeliberate. His tone is, throughout his first speech, at all times conciliatory. In the final eleven verses Eliphaz strikes an optimistic note, full of hope for Job's recovery;
a word of consolation to a man in pain:

> Happy the man whom God corrects.
> For though he wounds, he also binds up.
> He strikes but his hand also heals (5:17-18).

Granted the theological assumptions (of the dogma of divine
retribution) on which Eliphaz's speech is based, assumptions widely
accepted in Israelite theology, the speech (chapters 4&5) is a masterpiece of consolatory literature. It should be appreciated in its original context, and it deserves to be judged by the reader indep-
endently of Job's furious rejection of it in the following two chapters
(6&7). Eliphaz's remarks on human frailty are quite general, and at
no time does he specify any great sin on Job's part. What Eliphaz
says, in his first speech, is in line with the most insightful sayings of
the New Testament: 'If we say we have no sin, we deceive ourselves
and the truth is not in us' (1 Jn 1:8). It is in line also, of course, with
much in the Old Testament teaching. The fall of the Northern
Kingdom in 721BC and of Jerusalem in 587BC was attributed by the
great prophets to the sins of the people. The friends are not theological morons if viewed in the intellectual context of their own time.

Eliphaz and Job
Is Eliphaz telling Job, in the most diplomatic and oblique way he
can, that Job's past sins are the reason for God's punishing him
now? Or is he accepting Job's goodness and saying that all men,
frail creatures of the earth, can expect suffering and death as part of
the human condition, and that the only remedy is to turn to God for
deliverance?

The author of the Book of Job is a subtle theologian who wants the reader/listener to enter into the enigmas facing the thinking person, and so at many important points in his poem he gives us lines that could be interpreted in two different senses. (Think of 2:9, of 42:6).

If you read the opening lines of Eliphaz's first speech, in chapters 4 and 5 (he has two other speeches, chaps 15 and 22) you find him praising Job for all the good things he did in the past, and faulting him only for his present failure to hope in God. Later, in Eliphaz's third speech, he will specify four deliberate sins of Job, and call him a very wicked man (22:5), but by then the debate will have deteriorated on both sides, so that we can't be sure of the objectivity of Eliphaz. But in Eliphaz's first speech he is trying, we presume, to be positive and comforting although without the delicacy and tact required in the situation – he mentions Job's lack of patience. And it is precisely to this charge of impatience that Job makes the reply:

> 'What wonder if my words are intemperate? The arrows of
> Shaddai pierce me, and their poison goes into my spirit'
> (6:3b,4).

But Job doesn't regard these poisonous arrows of the Almighty as punishment for any sin. Job all the time protests his innocence. Why then does Shaddai inflict such pain on Job, a pain that drives him into frenzied speech?

Two lines of explanation are explored in chapters 4-7. One might be called the way of natural philosophy, the other the way of mythology. Both ways intermingle in the Book of Job.

The way of natural philosophy, the search of the wise men in the period before and during the emergence of Greek philosophy, to understand human existence, produced a great literature from Egypt to Mesopotamia which influenced Israel and of this influence the Book of Job and Ecclesiastes are the noblest fruits:

Man is by nature fragile, easily crushed by disease and early death. Man (Hb. *adam*) was formed from the dust (*'aphar*) of the soil (Hb. *adamah*), Gen 2:7. He therefore dwells in 'a house of clay' whose foundation is only the dust. He is, by nature, like a piece of pottery, easily broken. Job himself, when he sees his own pitiful wasted condition, actually feels like 'dust and ashes' (30:19).

This approach to human suffering is very special to Eliphaz (see 4:12-21, where he claims to have received a special illumination of this point), and to some extent also to Job (7:1-10) who speaks not just of his own misfortune but laments the fate of mankind whose life on earth is short and bitter, with no hope of life after death. (The Septuagint and Christian Fathers attributed to Job a belief in the resurrection, but the Masoretic text does not give any clear indication of such a belief.)

Man (and animals, Gen 2:19) are essentially 'earthlings' – made from the earth and, at death, returning to the earth. Job regards himself as 'moulded like clay' – and now, through illness, being reduced to dust again (10:9).

The deity is regarded as sometimes inflicting illness on an individual as a punishment for serious sin, but there are many instances where individuals suffering from serious skin diseases like Job's are not regarded as being thereby punished for sin. Take one example from Leviticus which uses the same word *shehin* ('boil') as in Job:

'And when there is in the skin … a boil that has healed, but in the place of the boil there appears a white swelling or a reddish-white spot, then it shall be shown to the priest, and the priest shall make an examination, and if it appears deeper than the skin and its hair has turned white, then the priest shall pronounce him unclean; it is the disease of leprosy, it has broken out in the boil …. But if the spot remains in one place, and does not spread, it is the scar of the boil, and the priest shall pronounce him *clean*'. (Lev 13:18-20,24).

The function of the priest in the Leviticus regulations was not to heal the sick person, nor to pray for the healing of the afflicted. It was to inspect the skin of the sick person and to pronounce him unclean or clean, and thereby unfit or fit for participation in the cultic assembly. There were no magical incantations for healing, as in Egypt and elsewhere, no recourse to witchcraft or quackery. A period of quarantine might be imposed. The interests of social hygiene were thus served by these regulations. When the leper was required to call out 'unclean', it was for the protection of others, and in no way implied he had been guilty of sin. The priest never required the afflicted leper to confess his sins or to pray for forgiveness.

When Eliphaz asks 'can man be *clean* (*tahor*) before his Maker?' (4:17b), he is using the same word as is used in Leviticus (13:17), for the person whose skin is declared clean. Eliphaz's rhetorical question is saying that no mere mortal is totally perfect in the eyes of his Maker – and he may be referring to physical as well as moral perfection. And Eliphaz's 'Can man be right (*saddiq*) before God' may also be taken to imply that even a good man (like Job) may unwittingly offend God, and thereby incur punishment, a punishment less than that reserved for the really wicked.

In the example from Leviticus we are mainly within the natural order of clinical observation and diagnosis of skin ailments, but in the first speech of Eliphaz another dimension is added: the mythological 'sons of Reseph'.

> 'For man is born for trouble, as the sons of Reseph fly upwards' (5:7).

Reseph is the god of pestilence in the Ugaritic pantheon, whose agents ('sons') fly up from the netherworld bringing disease and plague to the earth. The earth itself thus becomes contaminated, so that Eliphaz can ask the rhetorical question:

> Is it not from the soil that affliction springs?
> Is it not from the ground that trouble comes? (5:6).

(This verse can also be translated not as a question, but as a negative assertion giving the opposite sense – but that's the author of Job!) The very earth and the dust from which mankind springs and in which he lives is thus rendered hostile to man's health and well-being. The sorrows and sufferings of mankind thus may come from evil forces irrespective of man's character, good or bad, and thus Job's sufferings may not be due to any moral fault on his part.

What he should do, says Eliphaz, is to appeal to God for deliverance from this evil (5:8). Then Eliphaz explores further: even if it's God who is afflicting Job, the latter should accept the discipline of suffering, because the way the Almighty (Hb. *Shaddai*) works is to hurt you first and then heal you. No reason is given why Shaddai should hurt Job first and then heal him. The name Shaddai originally may have meant *mountain* or *steppe*, but in the Hebrew ear it sounded like a derivative of the verb *Shadad*, to destroy, despoil, – not a good omen, surely. But then Eliphaz wasn't an Israelite, but an Edomite who might have his theology tainted by the neighbouring mythologies. And Reseph, for good measure, although the god of pestilence, could be appealed to to call off his destructive sons, i.e. to heal!

Eliphaz's Shaddai thus reverses the sequence established by the Lord who 'gave and took away' (1:21); what we now have is Shaddai who takes away first, and then gives (health and prosperity). But no reasons for these strange combinations are given to the sufferer. In all Eliphaz's poem about Shaddai he is not attributing Job's misfortune explicitly to any specific sins of Job, nor does he invite Job to seek forgiveness from God for any sin. Nevertheless his talk about Job receiving the rebuke and the discipline of the deity (5:17) may seem to imply that Job must have sinned. But we have to recall that we are listening to the voice of Eliphaz, an

Edomite, whose notion of the deity had little of the exalted justice and mercy we look for in our own liturgy. The capriciousness of the gods in the non-Israelite mythologies showed itself in inflicting punishment *'without cause'*, to borrow a phrase from the God of the Prologue (2:3), which was also used later by Job to describe his perception of God's treatment of himself:

He crushes me for a trifle, and wounds me *without cause* (9:17), like a tyrannical father who corrects and disciplines a child who doesn't deserve it. In such a case, says Eliphaz, the only thing for the unhappy sufferer to do is to accept the 'discipline' and turn to God – the same God – for deliverance. This Job finds totally unacceptable.

When Job asks Eliphaz 'Show me where I have *erred'* (6:24) he uses the verb *shagah* which can apply to a moral fault or to an inadvertent sin or to any mistake. The context in chapter 6, with Job's reference to his own words as 'the utterance of a man without hope' (6:26), would suggest that Job's 'error' (in 6:24) was his intemperate language in the soliloquy which his three friends heard him speak seven days after they arrived to comfort Job, rather than any previous sins. Later, Job turns to God, and asks forgiveness 'if I have sinned' (7:20,21).

Eliphaz had tried to comfort Job but had failed. But his efforts were not without merit: he had commended Job's former concern for those depressed by the sorrows of life, although he spoiled it all by alluding to Job's present inability to help himself. He had assured Job that God would yet come to his rescue because it is only the wicked whom God destroys, whereas Job is a good man. The one sentence where Eliphaz may seem to have implied that Job was a sinner (5:7) may, in the mythological scenario of Ancient Near Eastern theology, be more a pointer to the imperfection of the deity than to that of Job. Eliphaz wants Job to endure the 'discipline' and to hope for deliverance. All in all, Job feels betrayed by the attitude of his friends; their words only further distressed him.

But Job was a hard man to please. He found fault with both God and man. From now on the so-called dialogue between Job and his three 'comforters' will be even less harmonious.

We do not have to wait long to meet a shocking application of the traditional doctrine of divine retribution: Job's children deserved their early death as a divine punishment for their sins. In Bildad's first speech he says to Job:

'Your sons sinned against God
So he delivered them into the power of their own iniquity' (8:4).

One is always amazed at how little notice is taken of the dead children of Job. He himself doesn't mention them during the poem, not even when confronted by Bildad's dreadful inference. We are left at the very end of the book with the insensitive thought that their replacement by ten other children somehow compensates for their lost lives.

Bildad moves quickly to his principal concern: If Job would only turn to God he would be delivered from his affliction. Bildad, in this, is in tune with long established theological consensus:

'Inquire now of the past generations.

And give heed to the experience of their fathers' (8.8).

But Bildad is not saying Job should admit his sins, nor that he should pray for forgiveness, nor that God should overlook some hypothetical sins of Job. Bildad's advice is that Job should seek God and pray that God would 'rouse himself' (8:6) and deliver Job from his sufferings:

'If you would seek after God,

And implore the favour of the Almighty,

Since (or If) you are pure and upright,

He will surely rouse himself for you,

And restore your righteous estate' (8:5,6).

Similar sentiments are expressed in Psalm 44:24(23), in which godly people, in spite of all their piety, have been crushed by terrible destruction, and so call on their God to 'rouse himself' (the same verb as Bildad uses) (see also Psalms 35 and 59 for the same theme). In neither case is there any imputation that the sufferer is sinful. Neither Eliphaz nor Bildad, in their opening speeches, nor the author of Psalm 44, impute any specific iniquity, not even 'a relatively trifling sin', to the sufferer.

The third friend, Zophar, however, regards Job as a sinner, although he does observe some caution by the use of 'if':

'If there is guilt in your hand, renounce it,

And do not let iniquity dwell in your abode' (11:14).

Then, says Zophar, Job will be amply restored. Zophar, who is most ungracious towards Job, seems to be chancing his arm, theologically, when he asserts that Job's present suffering is only a fraction of what his sin deserves (11:6c – presuming that this line is authentic, which some scholars doubt). Later on in the debate, of course, all reserve will be cast aside (as in 22:23), but 11:6c seems somewhat premature at this point. Whatever about this one line, Zophar, like the other two friends, finishes the first round of speeches on the hopeful note that Job will find divine deliverance.

In this they see themselves as his comforters.

But Job totally rejects their way of defending God at the expense of truth (13:7,8), and finds them 'miserable comforters' (16:2).

Summary:
Eliphaz's words of consolation
Chapters 4 & 5

a) 4:1-11 Grounds for hope: in the past Job helped many sufferers, encouraging them by his consoling words; now, however, when affliction strikes himself he is without resources. He should take heart and hope for restoration because he was always a good man, and, as he knows, it's only the wicked whom God destroys, not the good.

b) 4:12-21 All human beings (including Job) are imperfect in the eyes of their Maker. Man is a fragile structure of clay built on a foundation of dust, and so is easily crushed (by disease?) and broken (in death).

c) 5:1-16 The practical conclusion from all this is for Job not to indulge in passionate resentment against God, but to turn to God. The agents of Reseph (the god of pestilence) fly up from the nether-world bringing disease to the ground (Hb *adamah*), and so man (Hb *adam*), made from the clay, is born to trouble. Only God can deliver him.

d) 5:17-27 Consoling news for Job: If you accept the discipline of the Almighty (*Shaddai*) he will restore you. That's God's way: to wound but then to bind up and heal the wound. He'll then give you prosperity and a long and happy life.

Text:
Eliphaz's words of consolation

a)   4:1 Eliphaz the Temanite then replied:

2   'Should one dare a word, could you bear it?
     But who could be silent now?

3   Look, you have instructed many,
     Feeble hands you strengthened,

4   Your words encouraged the faint,
     Tottering knees you made firm,

5   But it befalls you and you falter;
     It strikes you, and you are dismayed.

6   Is not your piety your source of confidence,
     And your integrity your hope?

7   Consider, what innocent man ever perished,
     Or where have the righteous been destroyed?

8   I have observed that they who plant evil
     And sow trouble reap the same.

9   At a breath of God they perish,
     At a blast of his anger they vanish.

10   The lion may roar, the old lion growl,
     But the young lion's teeth are broken.

11   The lion perishes, robbed of prey,
     The lioness' whelps are scattered.

b)   4:12   Now a word came to me secretly,
            Just a whisper caught my ear.

     13   In a nightmare, in a trance,
            When heavy sleep falls upon men,

     14   Terror and trembling came upon me,
            All my bones shuddered.

     15   A breath passed over my face,
            The hair of my body bristled.

     16   It paused, but I could not discern it,
            Just a form before my eyes.
            A hush, then a voice I heard:

     17   'Can a mortal man be just before God?
            Can a man be clean in the sight of his Maker?'

     18   Even his servants he distrusts,
            Charges his angels with error.

     19   What then of those who dwell in houses of clay,
            Which are founded on dust,
            Who are crushed quick as a moth,

     20   'Twixt morning and evening shattered?
            They perish forever nameless,

     21   Their tent cord pulled up,
            They die without wisdom.

c)   5:1   'You may call now, but will anyone answer you?
            To which of the holy ones will you turn?

     2   Impatience kills the fool,
            Passion slays the simpleton.

     3   I have seen the fool strike root,
            But then his abode suddenly was accursed,

4   His children abandoned helpless,
     Crushed at the gate, defenceless.

5   His harvest the hungry consume,
     While the thirsty pant for their wealth.

6   Is it not from the soil that affliction springs?
     Is it not from the ground that trouble comes?

7   Man, indeed, is born for trouble,
     And the sons of Reseph fly upwards.

8   But, as for me, I would resort to God,
     To God I would commit my cause;

9   He it is who does great deeds inscrutable,
     Marvels beyond number,

10   Who gives rain to the earth,
     Sends water on the face of the field,

11   Who exalts the lowly on high,
     Lifts the mourners to safety.

12   He thwarts the plots of the crafty,
     So their hands attain no gain,

13   Catches the clever in their craftiness,
     And their wily schemes collapse.

14   By day they meet with darkness,
     Groping at noon as though it were night.

15   Thus he saves the simple from the sword,
     The poor from the clutch of the strong,

16   So that the humble have hope,
     And evil's mouth is stopped.

d)   17   Happy the man whom God corrects.
               Spurn not the discipline of the Almighty.

18 For though he wounds, he also binds up.
    He strikes but his hand also heals.

19 In six disasters he will save you,
    In seven no harm will befall you.

20 In famine he will save you from death,
    In war from the stroke of the sword.

21 From scourge of tongue you'll be hidden,
    Nor fear the robber when he comes.

22 You may laugh at plunder and famine;
    Wild beasts you need not fear.

23 You will have a pact with the stones of the field.
    Savage beasts will make peace with you.

24 You will know that your tent is secure,
    Inspect your home and miss nothing.

25 You will know a numerous progeny,
    Offspring like the grass of the ground.

26 You will come in full vigour to the grave,
    Like a sheaf of corn in its season.

27 This we have probed: 'tis true.
    Now hear it and know it yourself.'

Summary: Job's reply to Eliphaz
Chapters 6 & 7

a) 6:1-14 A Soliloquy: Job cries out in pain that the poisonous arrows of Shaddai (the Almighty) have pierced his flesh and deranged his mind so that his language is imprudent. It would be a consolation if he could die now knowing that he hadn't spoken against God.

b) 6:15-30 Job's friends have failed to bring him consolation; in fact they have upset him by criticising his outbursts without making allowance for his tormented state. 'Tell me plainly where I have erred' (6:24). Job is still convinced of his innocence.

c) 7:1-21 A direct address to God, complaining of God's harsh way of treating mankind. Man has only a short time to live on this earth, and then he vanishes forever. Why does God keep testing him with suffering? 'Even if I have sinned, why do you not forgive my offence' (7:21).

Text: Job's Reply to Eliphaz

a)   6:1   And Job answered and said:

2   Oh that my anguish were but weighed,
And my calamity laid in the balance together,

3   Then would it prove heavier than the sands of the sea,
Therefore have my words been frenzied;

4   For the arrows of the Almighty are within me,
Whose venom my spirit drinks up,
The terrors of God have troubled me.

5   Does the wild ass bray over grass?
Does the ox low over its fodder?

6   Is insipid food eaten without salt?
Or is there flavour in the white of egg?

7   My soul refuses to be quiet,
It is agitated by the sickness of my flesh.

8   Oh would that my request might come,
And that God would grant my hope:

9   That God may deign to crush me,
That He let loose His hand and cut me off!

10   Then it would still be my consolation –
And I would be steadfast in pain that spares not –
That I have not denied the words of the Holy One.

11   What is my strength, that I should wait?
And what is my end, that I should be patient?

12 Is my strength the strength of stones?
      And is my flesh of bronze?

13 Because there was no helper with me,
      So has prudence fled from me;

14 When his friend fails him who is in despair,
      He forsakes the fear of the Almighty.

15 My brethern are faithless as a torrent,
      As the bed of torrents that have passed away;

16 Which are turbid by reason of the ice,
      When the snow hides itself upon them;

17 What time it grows warm, they vanish away,
      When it is hot, they disappear from their place.

18 Caravans turn aside their ways,
      They come up through a waste, and are ready to perish;

19 The caravans of Tema look,
      The companies of Saba have hope;

20 They are disappointed, although they were confident,
      They come thither, and are confounded.

b)   22 Did I say: 'Give to me',
              Or 'offer a bribe for me out of your substance,'

         23 Or 'deliver me out of the hand of the adversary,'
              Or 'out of the hand of tyrants redeem me,'

        (21 That now ye are become heartless,
              Ye see a terror, and are afraid?)

         24 Teach me, and I will hold my peace,
              And let me know wherein I have erred;

         25 How pleasant are words of uprightness!
              But what avails reproof from you?

26   Do ye reckon words as worthy of reproof?
And the sayings of a desperate man as passion?

27   Nay, ye would cast lots upon the orphan,
Ye would bargain about your friend!

28   But now, be pleased to look at me,
Surely, I will not lie to your face;

29   Turn ye now, let there be no wrong.
Stay with me, my integrity is still intact.

30   Is there error in my tongue?
Cannot my palate discern falsehood?

7   1   Has not man hard service on earth?
And are not his days like the days of a hireling?

2   Like a slave who is eager for the shade,
And like a labourer who looks for his wages,

3   So have I been allotted months of woe.
And nights of trouble have been appointed to me.

c)   4   If I lie down, I say: 'When will it be (day)?'
If I rise: 'When will it be evening?'
And I am filled with agony till the twilight;

5   My flesh is clothed with worms and clods of dust,
My skin breaks up, and melts away;

6   My days are swifter than a weaver's shuttle,
And are come to an end without hope;

7   Oh remember that my life is but a breath,
My eyes shall not see happiness again;

8   The eyes of him that sees me shall not behold me,
Your eyes shall look for me, and I shall not be;

9   As the cloud comes to an end and vanishes,
    So he that goes down to Shoel shall not come up;

10 He shall return no more to his house,
    And his place shall know him no more.

11 I also will not refrain my mouth,
    I will speak in the anguish of my spirit,
    I will complain in the sorrow of my soul:

12 Am I a Sea, or a Dragon,
    That you set a watch on me?

13 If I say: 'My couch will give me relief,
    My bed will ease my complaint,'

14 Then you scare me with dreams,
    And terrify me with visions,

15 So that my soul prefers strangling,
    Death rather than my bones;

16 When I have pined away, I shall not come to life for ever,
    Let me alone, for my days are but a breath.

17 What is man, that you should magnify him?
    Or that you should regard him?

18 That you should visit him every morning?
    Test him at every moment?

19 How long till you look away from me?
    And let me alone till I swallow down my spittle?

20 If I sinned, what could I do to you,
    You watcher of men?
    Why have you set me as a mark for you,
    So that I am a burden to you?

21 And why do you not take away my sin?
    And remit my iniquity?
    For presently I shall lie down in the dust,
    And you will seek me, but I shall not be.

CHAPTER 3

The Hybris of Job

It is to the Book of Job more than to any other biblical work that many readers turn for consolation when confronted with the spectre of human suffering. The voice of Job, the innocent sufferer who cries out to God in endless lamentations for an explanation of his misery, has penetrated the inner ear of artists and theologians. And it is Job's voice, rather than that of the other participants in the dialogue, which continues ringing in our ears when we reach the end of the book, and this fact may be partly due to the chorus of commentators throughout the centuries who took Job's side in the argument and for whom the other participants offered either the 'miserable comfort' (of the friends) or windy rhetoric (Elihu) or irrelevant majesty of creation (the divine speech). The three friends, 'Job's comforters', are often caricatured as having achieved an effect totally at variance with their original intention. Elihu is presented as an intrusive voice with nothing original except his youthful self-confidence. Finally, the divine speech is hailed as a splendid nature-poem but without relevance to the problem of innocent suffering.

If this were a true evaluation of the Book of Job it would pose a serious question about the theological acumen of the author who could construct a debate in which only one speaker, namely Job, had all the truth on his side, and the five other participants had nothing of value to contribute. And it would certainly seem odd to allot such great length to all the non-Joban poems, in fact the bulk of the book, if they had nothing of value to say.

If Elihu is simply repeating what is found in the speeches of the friends and of the Lord, how could a great poet (or an intelligent editor) include them in his work? If the divine speech is irrelevant why is it there at all?

Is not the interest of any debate enlivened by the fact that something of value resides in either side of the argument, that there is a real contest between the two sides? If the value of the Book of Job is restricted to the speeches of Job, then the greater part of the Book is without serious purpose.

Could it be, however, that the Joban poet, even though his sympathy was with Job, felt that the other protagonists had some important insights which, while not refuting Job's arguments, were nevertheless of value in the discussion of human suffering? Our poet is an artist first and foremost.

He is not a theologian trained in systematic critico-historical methodology. And the function of an artist, as Anton Chekhov said, is not to solve problems but to present them correctly. This I believe, is what the Joban poet has done. Our poet has avoided neat endings, and allowed the various disputants to put their case at length, and has preferred to leave the debate end in inconclusiveness. The Book of Job is enhanced in value if each participant is given a hearing and treated with respect.

For many readers two factors have frequently tilted the balance of the argument in Job's favour: firstly, everyone feels sorry for the innocent sufferer Job, and, secondly, one sentence towards the very end of the book seems to settle the whole debate in favour of Job, when the Lord speaks to Eliphaz:

> I am angry with you and your two friends, because you have not spoken as you ought of me, as my servant Job has done (42:7).

Thus at the beginning of the book (where God praises the righteousness of Job) and at the end (42:7) where, again, the Lord approves of what Job has said, and disapproves of the friends' views, the reader is being influenced to side with Job and to devalue Job's opponents.

But a word of caution is needed here. The beginning and end of the book (in which Job is awarded highest divine acclaim) belong to the prose Prologue and Epilogue, and are quite different in style and content to the long poems. And if we attach great weight to what the Lord said in the prose sections we must also bear in mind that it is the Lord who speaks – at length – in the poem (chaps 38-41); and in the poem the Lord, far from praising Job's integrity, faults him on two accounts, viz. speaking ignorantly of God's designs in the world (38:2), and placing his own righteousness above that of the Lord's (40:8), thus committing the sin of hybris.

There is, in fact, a real and not just a verbal contradiction between the prose sections and the poetry in the Book of Job, a conflict which makes it unsafe to interpret some parts of the poem in the light of the prose. Thus Job's angry irreverence towards God in the poem can in no way be reconciled with his patient acceptance of his suffering in the Prologue. Likewise God's praise of Job in the

Epilogue cannot be reconciled with God's reprimand to Job in the poem.

If we turn for a moment to Ecclesiastes, we find a parallel phenomenon: in the beginning of that book the venerable name of king Solomon lends authority to the book, and in the Epilogue we are exhorted to observe the traditional piety of the Mosaic Law, but in the body of the book we find a more liberal outlook. Thus the Epilogue has:

> Fear God and keep his commandments; for this is the whole duty of man. For God will bring every deed into judgment, with every secret thing, whether good or evil (12:13, 14).

But in the corpus of the book we get advice far removed from the traditional:

> Rejoice, O young man, in your youth, and let your heart cheer you in the days of your youth; walk in the ways of your heart and the sight of your eyes (11:9).

> There is nothing better for a man than that he should eat and drink and find enjoyment in his toil (2:24).

Qohelet's liberal outlook caused disquiet within Judaism, as the dispute between Hillel (in favour) and Shammai (against) testify. The holy martyr Akiba spoke in its favour (early second century of Christian era) and the book was finally accepted into the Hebrew canon. But there is hardly any doubt that the two factors that tilted the balance in its favour are the attribution of Solomonic authorship and the pious sentiments of the Epilogue.[1]

With regard to the canonicity of Job, we have no written evidence of a similar debate in the period leading up to the formation of the Old Testament canon. But such a lack of evidence cannot hide the disquiet felt within the pious Jewish circles of more recent rabbinical theology. Interesting to see how the great scholar Moses Maimonides (1135-1204AD) reviews the anti-Job lobby:

> Our sages condemned the view of Job (which blamed God for man's misfortunes) as mischievous, and expressed their feeling in words like the following: 'Dust should have filled the mouth of Job'; 'Job wishes to upset the dish'; 'Job denied the resurrection of the dead'; 'He commenced to blaspheme'. But, said the sages, God ignored the sin of Job (in his utterances) because of the acuteness of his suffering on the principle that 'man is not punished for what he utters in his pain'.[2]

Maimonides' own solution to the meaning of God's approval of Job in 42:7 is that this approval applies only to the last two verses spoken by Job where Job 'abhors himself and repents in dust and ashes' (see 42:5, 6). This solution may be an easy way out for a sophisticated and wily exegete like Maimonides and the host of other commentators who followed him, but it places an enormous question mark on the great Joban poet whose hundreds of verses on the agony of Job are devalued suddenly in two short verses whose meaning is among the most obscure in the whole book, and which might well be translated in a less pessimistic tone than that given by Maimonides.[3]

There is no reasonable way of reconciling the Job of the prose (Prologue and Epilogue) with the Job of the poems; the former is patient and reverent, the latter is impatient and angry with God. The author obviously put his greatest effort into the poem with all its searching for the meaning of man's troubled existence. It is to the poem rather than to the prose we must go for the great thoughts of Job, daring and bold as they are. So daring and so bold that one may venture to think that without the pious sentiments of the Prologue and Epilogue to accompany them, the poems of Job might never have gained entry into the canon of scripture. The probability cannot be ruled out that both Job and Ecclesiastes depended on the pious sentiments found at the beginning and end of these two books to placate a largely traditionalist audience and to gain general acceptability within Judaism.

Still on this topic of the conflict between the Epilogue and the poem, we may point to the Lord's condemnation of the friends in 42: (Epilogue): 'you have not spoken well of me'. There is not one verse in the poems to which anyone can point in support of this condemnation. The friends never utter a word against God; they do utter words against Job, but not against God. Job, of course, accuses the friends of speaking falsely in favour of God, in being partial towards God, in taking God's side against him (13:7, 8). But is Job correct in making this accusation? By what criterion do we decide that Job is correct in his accusation? How can we assume that Job is fairly stating his opponent's state of conscience? Are exegetes to become partisan – taking Job's side against his friends? If we confine ourselves to the poem, we find no basis for taking Job's side against his friends.

When silence can be dangerous
To use God's commendation of Job in the Epilogue (43:7) to modify or contradict the reproaches made in the divine speech (38-41) is granting a superiority to the prose over the poetry which cannot be justified. But if the Lord's commendation of Job in the Epilogue is

referred back to the memorable statements in the Prologue in which Job twice blessed God's inscrutable ways, 'The Lord has given; the Lord has taken away. Blessed be the name of the Lord' (1:21; See 2:10), it would make good sense.

The whole tone and content of the Epilogue 42:7-10 takes us all the way back to the Prologue. In both prose sections, and only in those sections, is Job referred to as 'my servant' by the Lord (1:8; 2:2; 42:7) in both prose sections and only there is animal sacrifice regarded as a remedy for sin; and the only passages where Job speaks highly of God ('speaks rightly' 42:7) are in the Prologue (1:21; 2:8). When Job speaks in the poem about the Almighty's action in nature he 'selects examples illustrating God's unlimited and even irresponsible and destructive powers',[4] whereas the friends emphasise the beneficent aspects of the Almighty's actions.

Verse 42:7 is usually presumed to mean that the friends had spoken some words that were 'not correct' but if we look again at the text such a meaning does not impose itself. What the text says is negative not positive; it says they *didn't* speak what was correct, not that they did speak what was 'not correct'. The Lord said: 'I am angry with you … because you have *not spoken* about me what is correct (n^e *khonah*)' (42:7).

What many commentators do is to take the negative *lo'* ('not') away from the verb *dibbartem* ('spoken') and join to it n^e *khonah* ('correct'), and end up with a positive verb followed by negative noun. While such a re-arrangement is possible, it is by no means necessary, and the original text may well be interpreted as indicating that the friends remained silent – 'they did not speak' – when the Lord would have preferred them to have spoken correctly of his providence as Job had done.

The danger of silence. The children of Job had not spoken a word against God, and still their father offered sacrifice just in case they blasphemed mentally (1:5). The Prologue-Epilogue moves in a world where even silence can be dangerous. When Job's three friends arrived on the scene of his sorrows 'they raised their voices and wept' but they did not speak a word, and their silence lasted seven days. They expressed no religious attitude to the tragedy of Job – neither against God (as Job's wife may have done) nor in favour of God (as Job himself did). Could it be that their very silence, their failure to bless God, as Job had done, is the reason for the divine reproach (43:7)? Perhaps when 'they saw that his agony was very great' (2:13), they just could not honestly praise the Lord 'for all the evil he had inflicted on Job' (see 42:11).

And for this silence they incurred the wrath of the Lord. In the Prologue-Epilogue we are in the midst of a mythological scene where the deity is portrayed in a far from edifying manner: a deity who allows himself to be incited against a good man (Job) 'to destroy him without cause' (2:3), and where all Job's children can be wiped out as part of a divine wager with Satan (1:19). Verse 7 of chapter 42 belongs to this 'long ago of mythology' in which the anger of the deity is sometimes capricious, very different from the mature theology of the divine speech where no such anthropomorphisms appear.

When a good man sins

When God speaks out of the whirlwind he never speaks well of Job, and, in fact, reprimands him for his ignorance (38:2) and his arrogance (40:8). In this latter text, Job's sin of hybris is explicitly highlighted when God asks him: 'Would you annul my judgement, condemn me that you may be justified?'

Job, says God, had claimed to be more righteous than the deity. Job had claimed that he himself put down the wicked, but that God had failed to do so. God's reply to Job's charge is that human wickedness is so vast that Job, even if he had superhuman strength, would be unable to suppress it. God challenges Job to put on the garments of divine glory, and thus strengthened, to blast every proud man from the face of the earth:

> Have you an arm like God,
> Can you thunder with a voice like his?
> Deck yourself now with grandeur (ga'on) and majesty (gobhah)
> Be arrayed in glory and splendour.
> Let loose your furious wrath
> Look at every proud man and bring him low …
> Then I will acknowledge to you that your own right hand can save you (40:9-14).

While this pericope speaks mainly about Job's inability to put down the wicked, the final verse, strangely enough, avoids any claim that God himself puts down every proud man. In the divine speech God makes many claims for his all-powerful control of the cosmos and of natural creatures of the wild, but never once does he claim explicitly to put down all the wicked. And if there was one context in which such a claim could have suitably been made it was in the pericope just quoted. But this problem is not central to our present search for the sins of Job, to which we now return.

Much of Job's sorrow is related to the social alienation that fol-

lows his illness. The ultimate in humiliation for Job is the fact that
formerly he was held in the highest esteem by the nobility, but now
he is scorned even by the dregs of society, people whom he had
always held in disdain, or, as he himself so vividly puts it: 'men
whose fathers I would have disdained to put with the dogs who
kept my flock' (30:1). The whole passage which follows this verse
betrays Job's upper-class contempt for a whole category of misfor-
tunate poor whose only crime is their utter destitution and their
low social origin (30:8). In uttering these sentiments he contradicted
his own lofty sentiments on the equality of all men before the common Father:

> If I have ever rejected the plea of my slaves or of my slave-
> girls, when they brought their complaint to me,
> What shall I do if God appears?
> What shall I answer if he intervenes?
> Did not he who made me in the womb make them?
> Did not the same God create us in the belly (31:13-15).

This fine statement of principle Job extends even to his slaves
who, in ancient society, were generally regarded as outside the
administration of the law-courts. Job enunciates the principle as
applicable to all human beings, all children of the common Father.
But he now (30:8) excludes those wretched poor whom he disdains,
and gives a contemptuous description of their starvation-diet (salt-
worth and root of broom), their uncouth language, and cave-men
existence, outcasts from civilised communities (probably because
they stole some food to stay alive):

> Gaunt with want and hunger
> they plucked saltworth ...
> and the root of broom for their food.
> Driven from the society of men,
> pursued like thieves
> they lived in gullies and ravines, holes in the earth, and rocky
> clefts.
> They howled like beasts among the bushes,
> vile and men of no name (30:3-8).

Of these men Job says he refused to employ them in his service
precisely because of their lack of physical strength to do a good
day's manual work for him. Job 'had nothing to gain from the
strength of their hands' (30:2). Here Job is in direct conflict with the
social conscience of Israel as enshrined in Leviticus 25:35, 'If thy
brother becomes impoverished and weak of hand, you shall maintain him'. In spite of the textual difficulties, the picture is disturb-

ing, both in its description of utter destitution of outcasts from society, and in Job's adding his own disdain, and his refusal to employ them precisely because of their pitiful weakness. There is, I suppose, only one other passage in Job which speaks in similar terms of the physical hunger and weakness of outcasts and this also occurs on the lips of Job, but with one significant difference: Job now faults God for not listening to their cry:

> They (the wicked) jostle the poor out of the way,
> the destitute huddle together, hiding from them.
> The poor rise early like the wild ass,
> when it scours the wilderness for food,
> but though they work till midnight
> their children go hungry.
> Naked and bare they pass the night;
> in the cold they have nothing to cover them ...
> they tread the winepress but themselves go thirsty ...
> like wounded men they cry out;
> but God pays no heed to their prayer (24:4-12).

Some land-owners did employ these poor men but their reward was insufficient to maintain them. God did not heed the cry of these, says Job (24:12), but Job would have no association at all with them. (Were they gypsies or 'travellers'?)

Job can criticise God for something he himself boasts about. Job's sin is rooted in his position of an immensely wealthy landowner who owns male and female slaves, vast herds and lands, and is also highly respected as a civic leader and judge.

The author of the poem (as distinct from the prose) thus places on the lips of Job himself sentiments which betray his arrogance and sense of self-importance and his disdain for others. In fact, the simple matter of walking down the street becomes, for Job, an exercise is hybris: he accepts the obsequious respect of the whole hierarchy of society from ordinary youngsters who keep out of sight, up to the nobility who look up to him as if he were their king. And once he had spoken at their assembly, no one spoke again. When he smiled on them 'they lost their gloomy looks' (29:7-25). In this and similar passages, the poet is letting Job display his enormous pride – a pride which is shaken only in the presence of God's mighty work in nature – when Job eventually realises how silly all human posturing becomes before God. Thus Job's first reply to God 'I am little' (Hb *qalloti*) is of immense importance in his spiritual recovery from hybris (40:4). When scholars fail to find the divine speech relevant to the problem of innocent suffering they are correct, but when they see the divine speech as irrelevant to the problem of Job they may be missing a very important aspect of the poet's way of presenting Job, viz. that Job's pride is part of his own problem. Much of Job's suffering is caused by his former self-importance, and the humiliation which he now suffers stems from the low opinion in which he is presently held by many because of his misfortune.

Job is always conscious of his princely position at the top of the hierarchy; he uses the abstract noun – very rare in Old Testament – n^e dibhah, 'my station as a prince' (30:15). When God ironically challenges him to deck himself out in pride and majesty (40:8) the terminology used is highly indicative of the Lord's understanding of Job's exaggerated self-esteem. The verb ga'ah, 'to be exalted', 'to lift up one's head', can be used in the sense of 'being proud'; and its noun ga'on, as well as the noun gobhah, both of which may properly be used of God's majesty, are used of Job's pride.

The sin of human pride was particularly offensive to the piety of Israel which saw in it man's desire to be equal to God. Perhaps Israel's most vivid abhorrence of this sin finds its expression in the Hebrew of Sirach:

How can he who is dust and ashes be proud?
even in life his bowels decay (Sir 10:9).

In his pride frail man forgets his limitations and tries to scale the heavens and compete with God. Job had placed his own righteousness higher than the Lord's (40:8).

Job's pride also manifested itself in his relationship with his fellow human beings, as some of his own words revealed (30:3-8); and it is at this level that his three friends and Elihu fault Job. But none of the friends deny that Job has many good qualities to his credit. Eliphaz, who is the first of the three to speak, is happy to recall Job's many kindnesses to those who were in distress, and even uses this fact as a good reason why Job should be hopeful of a return to God's favour (chaps 4, 5).

However, even a good man may slip unwittingly into evil ways, Eliphaz politely reminds Job. Human nature is fragile, not only at the physical level (as Job discovers during his illness) but also at the moral level (but Job never admits to any moral fault).

The hidden sins of Job
The term 'hidden sins' is very rare in Old Testament literature, but the concept is important for an appreciation of what the friends think about Job. Perhaps, if we turn first to Psalm 51, one of the great penitential psalms, it will illuminate the manner. The

Psalmist, like the three friends, acknowledges that sinfulness is an all-pervasive reality in human life and that man stands in need of divine enlightenment in order to detect the evil that dwells in the depths of his heart:

> Behold, I was brought forth in iniquity,
> and in sin did my mother conceive me.
> Behold, thou desirest truth in the inward being;
> therefore teach me wisdom in my secret heart (Ps 51:5, 6).

Verse 6 just quoted presents considerable difficulty for translators. Kissane's translation of the verse (which is v. 8 in the Hebrew) is 'Behold, truth in which thou delightest was obscured', and this translation preserves the word-order of the original and gives the general sense of man's conscience having to contend with dark recesses of his heart, the seat of evil tendencies of which he is not fully aware. This reality of sin requires not just human resourcefulness to remedy it, but also God's purifying grace (v. 9 Hebrew), and leads to the prayer for a cleansing of the heart:

> A clean heart create for me, O God,
> and make new within me a steadfast spirit (v. 12 Hebrew).

Kissane's comment on this verse is: 'In certain conditions, God's will is hidden from man, and so through ignorance of the law one may sin and thus deserve chastisement. It is for this reason that one prays to God to show him the way lest he sin in the future.'[5]

Perhaps more illuminating than the difficult verses from Psalm 51 is the story of David's repentance after his sin with Bathsheba. The enormity of David's double sin of the adultery with Bathsheba and the murder of her husband does not seem to have distressed him until the prophet Nathan invited him to pass judgment on the rich man who stole the ewe lamb from its humble owner. When David condemned the rich man Nathan said to David: 'You are the man,' and David replied: 'I have sinned against the Lord.' The crimes of the very rich man, who had more flocks than he needed, and the crimes of David, rich and powerful king, could escape public condemnation in the societies where they reigned supreme. The social structures favoured the exploitation of the lowly, and the conscience of the rulers was not greatly disturbed by deeds which were often connived at by high society. But the prophet, speaking for God, brought to light the obscured regions of the heart.

Job's friends also frequently admonish Job that his illness is God's way of revealing to him sinful aspects of his conduct into which his vast wealth and privilege had led him unwittingly. The only sins of which the friends accuse Job arises directly from his

high social position and class-consciousness. They are not denying
that Job (like David) has a lot to his credit, but they insist that evil
has crept into his attitude towards certain distressed people in his
society. And Elihu says:

> If he declares before all men, 'I have sinned, turned right into
> wrong, and thought nothing of it,' then he saves himself from
> going down into the pit, he lives and sees the light. All these
> things God may do to a man, again and yet again bringing
> him back from the pit (of death) to enjoy the full light of life
> (33:27-30).

Job may feel that he is clean in the sight of God, but this, in itself,
is no guarantee that evil is not hidden in his heart – evil which God
can see. When Job says that God can see he is innocent he is presuming to have God's knowledge. This is the point which Zophar
advances against Job:

> And shalt thou say, 'My doctrine is pure,
> And I am clean in thy sight'?
> But oh that God might speak,
> And open his lips with thee,
> And declare to thee the secrets of wisdom.
> It is because he is wonderful in counsel and knowledge
> that he requireth thee to thy iniquity (11 4-6). (Kissane)

God, if he spoke to Job about his hidden faults, would be revealing 'the secrets of his (Job's) heart' which only divine wisdom knows
clearly and which God can make clear to Job if he is humble enough
to accept correction.

Elihu clearly emphasises that certain evils almost inevitably go
with high office and are recognised as sins against God only when
illness strikes down the exalted:

> And with kings on this throne,
> He (God) makes them reign for ever, and they are exalted.
> But if they be bound in fetters,
> And held fast in the bonds of affliction,
> Then he declareth to them their work,
> And their offence, that they have behaved proudly
> And he opens their ear to instruction,
> And commands that they turn from iniquity
> If they hearken…they shall live out their days in happiness (36:7-12).

The temptations of the man in high office are insidious, and they
undermine his integrity without his being fully aware of the corruption that is taking place in his heart: the unlimited plenty spread
out before him, and the generous table and hospitality which many

people offer the great man can influence his judgment when important matters (of state, of property rights, etc.) have to be decided:

> If you eat your fill of a rich man's fare when you are occupied
> with the business of the law, do not be led astray by lavish
> gifts of wine, and do not let bribery wrap your judgment
> (36:16-19 NEB).

It is in this context that important men like the Prince of Tyre
(Ezechiel 28), kings in their arrogance (36:7ff), and Job in his pride,
are given a chance to repent of their 'hidden faults', hidden, not so
much from others who may indeed have to suffer from their arrogance, but from the culprit himself who, in his exaltation, was carried away by hybris.

Confirmation of this approach is, in part, to be found in the only
pericope in the divine speech in which the Lord speaks directly about
Job, and accuses Job of the supreme hybris of exalting his own
righteousness above that of God (40:8) – the temptation of frail man
carried away by his temporary success to measure himself against
the omnipotent Lord of the cosmos.

Job himself is sensitive to the danger of partiality that his own
high position in society poses in the context of his being involved in
litigation against a weaker opponent:

> If I have raised my hand against the innocent knowing that
> men would side with me in court (31:21 NEB).

And also that his great wealth is a fascinating attraction, which
could overpower his moral motives:

> If I have put my faith in gold
> and my trust in the gold of Nubia,
> If I have rejoiced in my great wealth
> and in the increase of riches (31:24, 25).

Job, of course, denies having succumbed to any of these temptations, but his friends are not so sure that he was always successful.
Job himself admits that there were times when his male and female
slaves expressed grievances against him (31:13) but feels that he
met their claims. In one verse only does Job seem to admit the fact
of his misdeeds, but he spoils his confession by claiming superiority
over other men who prefer to hide their guilt from the public: 'Have
I ever concealed my misdeeds as men do …?' (31:33a).

One is reminded of the parable told by Jesus of the two men who
went up to the Temple to pray, and the Pharisee who thanked God
that he was 'not like the rest of men'. Job's disdain for others is built
into his protestations of integrity, and this feature of his character
tilts the balance against him in his argument with his three friends.

Another point of comparison with the Pharisee of the parable is Job's boasting about his work of supererogation. The Pharisee in the parable gave tithes of all he possessed – something he was not obliged by law to do. Job, in a quite remarkable utterance, claims to have exercised an amazing and uncalled for degree of self-control in the matter of sexual purity:

> I have come to terms with my eyes, never to take notice of a
> girl (31:1).

The Law did not forbid a man to look at an unmarried woman, and the later rabbinic blessing to be recited on seeing a beautiful woman probably represents the wholesome appreciation of feminine beauty going back many centuries: 'Blessed be God who has such in his world'. However there were also to be found, in rabbinic times – and presumably before that – attitudes of rigid self-restraint in this regard too, including the legend of Abraham's unawareness of the beauty of his wife Sarah. Such excessive circumspection, however, seems at variance with the Wisdom tradition of Israel, and one cannot escape the impression that the poet who composed 31:1 felt that Job was protesting too much.

Exegetes who change the word 'girl' ($b^e tulah$) in 31:1 to 'calamity' ($n^e bhalah$) have no warrant for it either in the Hebrew text or in the versions. Kissane's reason for thus amending the text is, partly, on the basis that 'the reference to a "virgin" in verse 1 would be better in place in connection with adultery (which is treated in verse 9). Robert Gordis' reply to such a desire for re-arranging verses on the grounds of relevance is worth quoting: 'The absence of Western coherence characterises all the biblical law codes' (p 545).

In this connection one is reminded of the overbearing attitude of Leo Tolstoy's friend and mentor Chertkov, who in the later years of the great novelist's life would arrive at Yasnaya Polyana in the morning while Tolstoy was writing. He entered, peered over the old man's shoulder, read what he was writing, approved, criticised: 'It would be better to change that passage'. 'Ah, you think so?' murmured Tolstoy, adding 'I thought that was what I wanted to write', but then, irritated and uncomfortable, he gave in.

While one must admit that Chertkov had an enormous mastery of Tolstoyism and was held in awe for this even by the great writer himself, one may be forgiven for being happier with the original thought of the master – be he Tolstoy or the poet of Job.

The dangers of Job's wealth

A basic principle in the friends' argument against Job is that human nature in all human beings, including Job, is frail, not only physically (as Job accepts, see chap 3) but also morally, so that evil can easily creep into a good man's thoughts and deeds. As Eliphaz puts it:

> What is frail man that he should be innocent, or the child of woman that he should be justified? If God puts no trust in his holy ones, and the heavens are not innocent in his sight how much less so is man? (15:14).

Neither in his first or second speech does Eliphaz mention any specific sin of Job. Only in his third and final speech does he get down to specifics when he lists four faults of Job, all related to Job's great wealth and social prestige. The four are: depriving his own kinsman, 'brother' (some mss have a plural here instead of a singular) of his clothing taken in pledge, and doing this 'without due cause'; refusing water to someone who was thirsty; refusing bread to someone who was hungry; not helping windows and orphans:

> Without due cause you take a brother in pledge,
> you strip men of their clothes and leave them naked.
> When a man is weary, you give him no water to drink
> and you refuse bread to the hungry.
> Is the earth then the preserve of the strong,
> and the domain of the favoured few?
> Widows you have sent away empty-handed,
> orphans you have struck defenceless (22:6-9).[6]

Job, of course, denies these charges; but who is right, the friends or Job? Could it be that while Job had done many good deeds in his long life he had also on occasion fallen victim to human frailty? The four sins of which the friends accuse him are all related to wealth. Job is never accused of adultery, fornication, perjury, idolatry. Like Keret, the good king of Khubur in Ugaritic literature, the only faults of which he is accused related to the unjust administration of his vast properties, and this only inadvertently, and, in Keret's case during a period of illness. To say that Eliphaz simply invents the four sins of Job finds no basis in the text. Job himself admits to an instinctive disdain for certain lower classes of society (31:1-5), and this ungracious trait may be at work in subtle ways in his behaviour. Lord Acton's aphorism about power tending to corrupt, and absolute power corrupting the holder absolutely is not far from the Wisdom tradition in Israel. Speaking of the danger of great wealth (and using for the first time an Aramaic term *mammon*, 'Wealth', 'gold') a later (deutero-canonical) work doubts if anyone can escape its corruption:

Happy the rich man who has remained free from its taint, and has not made gold his aim.

Show us that man, and we will congratulate him,
has anyone ever come through this test unscathed? (Sir 31:8).

Ezechiel's oracle against the king of Tyre is closer in time to the author of Job, and speaks of the prince who, like Job, was favoured by God and 'was blameless' from the beginning until he was corrupted by wealth (Ezech 28:15-17).

The friends, however, are always hopeful that Job will find his way back to God's favour. They generally (though not always) avoid applying the term 'wicked' to Job. An interesting clash of opinions on this very point arose between Mgr Edward Kissane of Maynooth, whose splendid commentary on Job appeared over fifty years ago (1939), and M. Pope's learned *Job* (1965). In an unusually emotive passage, Pope criticises Kissane's benign view of the friends:

The suggestion (by Kissane) that … he (Job) does not belong to the category of the really wicked, is casuistry surpassing that of the friends.[7]

The position of the friends (and of Elihu) may have more subtlety than it has been credited with. The friends are at fault for denying the facts of experience in regard to the worldly success of some wicked people, and also for assuming that suffering is always a consequence of sin. But this doesn't mean they have nothing of value to offer.

If one may be permitted to take a sympathetic view of the friends' arguments one might select the following scoring-points in their favour:

1) Against Job, who never admits to any specific fault, the friends assert that all men are frail, not merely physically (as Job agrees in chap 3) but also morally. In this the friends are in tune with the bulk of religious thinking both inside Israel and beyond. See above, 15:14-16 for one example out of many.

2) Even a good man (like Job) who has helped many people in their distress may inadvertently fall into sinful ways. The only sinful ways of which the friends accuse Job are all related to his great wealth and high position in society (22:6-9).

3) If the Lord chastises the sinner with suffering, this suffering may have the beneficial effect of leading the sinner to become aware of his 'hidden' faults, to confess his sins to God, and to receive God's forgiveness and be restored to health again. This thought was expressed at the very outset of the dialogue in Eliphaz's first speech:

Happy the man whom God corrects.
Therefore do not reject the discipline of the Almighty (5:17).

4) But if the sinner, in spite of God's warning persists in his sins and becomes hardened in his wickedness, he will die (36:11, 12). Job disputes this point (21:29-34). The friends, and Elihu, always consider Job's case with hope for his eventual return to health and prosperity. They do not regard him as a hardened sinner. Only in his final speech does Eliphaz go too far in speaking of Job's wickedness (22:5), but this is an exceptional breach of his usual good manners.

Conclusion

The Job poem is the most searching analysis of human arrogance in the Bible, and arguably in all ancient literature. It studies the hybris of Job as the friends and Elihu saw it, rooted in the wealth and social eminence of Job, and leading him into anti-social behaviour. It also studies the hybris of Job as the Lord in the divine speech saw it, namely as placing man's righteousness above that of God. It studies the hybris of Job as formulated by the very words of Job himself in his boasting about his sinlessness – especially in his litany of self-praise in chapter 31, in his disdain of the lower classes (30:1-5), and in his vilification of the friends for their refusal to take his side against God, as if their loyalty to Job should supersede their loyalty to their religious convictions. Job says:

> Loyalty is due from his friends to one who loses faith in the Almighty (6:14 NEB).

This extraordinary sentence may be the earliest formulation in Hebrew literature of the principle that loyalty to friends is the highest of human values. A loyalty more basic than even loyalty to God – if we are to interpret Job as the NEB and other have done.[8]

The friends, however, refuse to follow Job in his condemnation of God. They offer him the consolation of their tears, but their first loyalty is to God.

On the theodicy issue, Job's thesis stands: the wicked are not always punished on this earth. The Lord, when at last he spoke from the whirlwind, did not contradict Job on this. Neither did the Lord condemn Job for any of the anti-social sins mentioned by the friends. But, to be precise, the Lord doesn't mention this point one way or the other. What the Lord does reproach Job for is his incompetence to pass judgment on the complexities of the Creator's ways (38:2) and his hybris in placing his own righteousness above the Lord's (40:8). The only voice that Job really listens to is the Lord's from the mighty works of nature. Job's reply (40:4; 42:2-6) shows he has learnt the truth about himself, and has discarded his pride but not his reason.

Notes

1. See Crenshaw, James, L., *Ecclesiastes* (London 1980), 52.
2. Maimonides, M., *Guide for the Perplexed*, trans M. Friedlaender (New York 1956), 300.
3. See O'Connor, Daniel, J., 'Job's Final Word – "I am Consoled' ...", *ITQ* 50 (1983/84), 181-97.
4. Diver-Gray, *Job* (Edinburgh 1921), 85.
5. Kissane, E. J., *The Book of Psalms* (Dublin 1953), 228.
6. These four sins of Job seem like the antitheses of the virtues of Boaz the wealthy land-owner, who was motivated by bonds of kinship to give water to the thirsty, and grain to the hungry, and to help the poor widow Ruth from the land of Moab (Ruth 2:8-16).
7. Pope, M., *Job* (New York 1965), 36.
8. See Habel, Norman C., *The Book of Job* (Cambridge 1975), 41.

Summary: Job's final speech
Chapters 29, 30, 31.

In this magnificent soliloquy, Job first looks back to the good old days when he was the leading light in society and an outstanding benefactor to the poor and downtrodden (29).

Then he looks at his present sufferings and humiliation when even the dregs of humanity look down on him (30). Finally he swears, in powerful oaths before God, that he is totally innocent (31).

Interwoven throughout is Job's firm conviction of his own supreme importance and virtue; his hybris shows itself in his disdain for the lower classes, in his total disregard for his wife's dignity (31:9,10), and in his presumption to pass adverse judgment on God.

Job had helped the afflicted who had called to him; now when he calls out to God for help, he gets no answer (30:20-25). Job claims he is more righteous than God. (The *manner* of Job's claim may be offensive to the pious ears of his friends, but it will be taken seriously by the Lord (40:8) and by all subsequent theology).

In spite of his hard words against God, it is to God that Job looks for justice in his final request that a member of the divine tribunal would hear his case and grant him an acquittal written on a scroll that Job would proudly wrap over his shoulder and around his head in a flamboyant gesture for all to see (31:35-37). See chapter 4, *Reverence and Irreverence*, for Job's lawsuit.

Text: Job's final speech
Chapters 29, 30, 31.

Remembering the good times

29   1   And Job answered and said:

     2   Oh that I were again back in the old times,
          In the days when God watched over me!

     3   When His lamp did shine above my head,
          By His light I walked through the darkness;

     4   As I was in the prime of my life,
          When God put a hedge about my tent;

     5   When the Almighty was still with me,
          And my young men round about me;

     6   When my steps were washed with butter,
          And the rock poured me out rivers of oil;

     7   When I went out to the gate of the city,
          When I set up my seat in the market-place

     8   The young men saw me, and hid themselves,
          And the old men rose up and stood;

     9   Princes refrained from speaking,
          And laid their hand on their mouth;

   10   The voice of the chiefs was hushed,
          And their tongue clave to their palate;

   11   When the ear heard me, it blessed me,
          And when the eye saw me, it gave testimony of me;

12 For I delivered the poor who cried out for aid,
    And the orphan who had no helper;

13 The blessing of the destitute came upon me,
    And I made the heart of the widow joyful.

14 I put on righteousness, and it clothed me,
    My justice was a cloak and a diadem;

15 I was eyes to the blind,
    And I was feet to the lame,

16 And I was a father to the poor;
    And the cause of one I knew not I examined,

17 And I broke the jaws of the unjust,
    And from his teeth I rescued the prey;

18 And I said: 'Like the reed shall I die,
    And like the palm-tree shall I multiply my days;

19 My root is spread out to the waters,
    And the dew lodgeth on my branches;

20 My glory is fresh in me,
    And my bow is renewed in my hand.

21 They listened to me, and waited,
    And they kept silence for my opinion,

22 And after I had spoken, they spoke not again;
    And upon them my words fell gently

23 And they waited for me as for the rain,
    And they opened their mouths, as for the spring rain;

24 I smiled at them, when they had lost heart,
    If I were pleased, they did not dissent.

25 I used to choose their way, and sit as chief,
    And dwelt as a king in the army,
    As one who comforts mourners;

But now, my harp is tuned to mourning
30   1   But now, they laugh at me,
              Men who are younger in years than I,
          Whose fathers I would not have deigned
              To put with the dogs who kept my flock!

2 As for the might of their hands – what use was it to me?
    In them was all vigour perished,

3 Exhausted with want and famine!
    Who gnawed the food of waste and desolation,
Who plucked saltwort and the leaves of shrubs,
    Whose food was the root of the broom;

5 From the society of men were they driven out,
    Men cried against them as against a thief;

6 In a cliff of the valleys they had to dwell,
    In holes in the ground and rocks;

7 Among the bushes they whimpered,
    And under the nettles they huddled together;

8 An ignoble, nameless brood,
    That were cut off out of the land!

9 And now I am become their song,
    And I am become a byword to them;

10 They abhor me, they stand aloof from me,
    And from my face they have not withheld spittle;

11 Because He stripped off my excellency and afflicted me,
    The bridle from their mouth they have cast away;

12 At the right hand the brood rise up,
    They let loose slander against me;
They have cast up their roads of ruin,

13 They have pulled down my paths, for my undoing;
    They prevail, there is none to restrain them,

14 As through a wide breach they advance.
    Under a storm I was rolled about,

15 Terrors were turned upon me;
    And my honour was chased as by the wind,
And like a cloud my welfare passed away;

16 And now my soul pours itself out within me,
      Days of affliction take hold of me;

17 By night my bones are pierced,
      And the pains that gnaw me take no rest;

18 With His great might He seized my garment,
      Like the collar of my tunic He girded me;

19 He hurled me into the mire,
      And I am become like dust and ashes.

20 I cry to you, and you answer not,
      I stand, and you regard not;

21 You are changed to a cruel one towards me,
      With the might of your hand you assail me;

22 You lift me up, on the wind you make me ride,
      You toss me about with a storm;

23 Yea, I know that you will bring me to death,
      The house of meeting of all the living;

24 Surely, against the needy one put not forth the hand,
      If in his calamity he cry out for redress;

25 Verily, I did weep for one whose day was sad,
      My soul did grieve for the poor!

26 Though I looked for good, yet evil came,
      And I hoped for light, but there came darkness;

27 My bowels boil, and rest not,
      Days of affliction have come upon me;

28 I walk about sorrowful, and not in affluence,
      I rise up in the assembly, I cry out;

29 My skin is black upon me,
      And my bones are burnt with fever-heat;

30   I am brother to the jackals,
     And companion to the ostriches;

31   And my harp is tuned to mourning,
     And my pipe to the voice of weepers.

I swear I am innocent

31   1   I made a covenant with mine eyes,
        Never to take notice of a girl,

     2   And what is the portion of God from above?
        And the heritage of the Almighty from on high?

     3   Is not ruin for the wicked?
        And adversity for the doers of evil?

     4   Does he not see my ways?
        And number all my steps?

     5   Or have I walked with vanity?
        And has my foot hasted towards deceit?

     6   Let him weigh me in a true balance,
        And let God know my integrity!

     7   If my step has turned from the way,
        And my hand has gone after my eyes,
     Or if aught has cleaved to my hands,

     8   Let me sow, and let another reap,
        And let my offspring be rooted out!

     9   If my heart has erred concerning a woman,
        And I have lain in wait at my neighbour's door,

   10   Let my wife grind for another,
        And let others bow down upon her!

   11   For that would be licentiousness,
        That would be an offence to be punished by the judges.

12 For that would be a fire which consumes to Abaddon,
    An offence that would burn up all my increase.

13 If I rejected the right of my man-servant,
    Or my maid-servant, when they contended with me,

14 What then should I do, when God should rise up,
    And when He visited, what should I answer Him?

15 Did not He that made me in the womb make him also?
    Did not the Same fashion us in the belly?

16 If I withheld from the poor what they desired,
    And made the eyes of the widow to languish,

17 And have eaten my morsel alone,
    And the orphan ate not thereof –

18 For from my youth He brought me up like a father,
    And from my mother's womb He did guide me.

19 If I saw one destitute, without clothing,
    Or that a poor man had no covering,

20 Surely, his loins blessed me,
    And with the fleece of my sheep he was warmed;

21 If I waved my hand against the orphan,
    Because I saw my help in the gate,

22 Let my shoulder fall from the shoulder-blade,
    And my arm be broken from its sockets!

23 For the terror of God would come upon me,
    And before His majesty I could not endure.

24 If I have made gold my confidence,
    Or said to fine gold: My trust!

25 If I rejoiced because my substance was great,
    And because my hand had got much,

26 If I beheld the sun when it shone,
    And the moon moving in splendour,

27 And my heart was secretly seduced,
    So that my hand kissed my mouth,

28 This would have been a crime before the law,
    And I should have betrayed God on high.

29 If I rejoiced in the ruin of him that hated me,
    Or exulted when calamity overtook him –

30 And I allowed not my palate to sin,
    By asking his life with a curse.

31 Verily, the men of my household have said:
    Who can show one who has not been sated with his meat?

32 The stranger did not pass the night in the street,
    I opened my door to the wayfarer;

38 If my land cried out against me,
    And the furrows thereof wept together,

39 If I ate of the produce thereof without payment,
    And caused the owners thereof to expire,

40 Instead of wheat let thistles grow,
    And noxious weeds instead of barley!

33 If I concealed my transgressions as men do,
    By hiding my guilt within my bosom,

34 Because I feared the crowd of the city,
    And the scorn of families terrified me,
So that I remained quiet, and went not out of doors –

Job's last request
35 O, that I had one to hear (my case)
    Here is my taw (i.e. my last word):
Let the Almighty answer me.
And the scroll which my adversary has written –

36 Surely on my shoulder I would carry it,
      And wear it like a crown on my head;

37 I would give him an account of all my life
      I would present it like a prince.

    Job's words are ended.

CHAPTER 4

A lesson from nature

When at last the Lord speaks to Job, one might expect to hear words of tenderness softly spoken bringing consolation to a long-suffering innocent man. But no. From the start we experience the whirlwind, the storm, the mighty forces of nature, some of them hostile to man's existence. One such storm had swept across the desert and killed all Job's children. Small wonder then that Job is twice over-awed and silenced by the experience of the voice from the wilderness (40:4,5 and 42:1-6).

The background from which the Lord speaks is twice referred to as the whirlwind, viz. at the beginning of each of the two divine speeches (38:1; 40:6). This term points to the threatening nature of some aspects of the natural world which Job needs to be aware of, and which are all part of the Lord's creation, and are used to teach Job the truth about himself and the world he lives in.

In the divine speeches the Lord is like a master of wisdom imparting instruction to a contentious opponent, Job, in a debate on theodicy that has already been going on too long.

The divine speeches open with a mighty salvo: all the wonder of heaven and earth, stars and sea, light and darkness are arranged before the eyes of Job. These mysteries of inanimate nature are beyond the understanding of Job, an intimation to Job that he is not in a position to pass judgment on the ways of the Creator – a theme anticipated in the great poem in chapter 28 on the inaccessibility of wisdom. (38:1-38)

Then the Lord turns to living creatures – the lion, the raven, the mountain-goat: creatures of God which are uncared for by man, but which are the objects of God's concern. God, depicted as cruel by Job, now begins to adduce numerous examples from the animal world of his providential regard for his creatures.

The poem on the wild ass (39:5-8) takes the argument a step further, and it is the first example of animal psychology in the divine speech. The innate love of freedom which the wild ass has makes it spurn man's desire to subjugate him. Thus begins an oblique criticism of human greed, and the first example in the Bible of animal liberation, in which the Lord takes the side of the animal, 'whose home I (God) have made in the wilderness' (39:6). This animal disdains the noisy city of man and refuses to accept man as its taskmaster (39:7).

This poem is followed by a similar one on the wild ox. Job, in his earlier opulence, owned many asses and oxen. Part of Job's misfortune was his loss of his farm-animals. This poem reminds him how man's greed for further expansion of his animal herds by capturing them in the wild and domesticating them is frustrated by their God-given instinct for freedom:

> Does the wild ox consent to serve you,
> Does it spend the night in your stall?
> Can you harness its strength with ropes,
> Or will it harrow the furrow after you? (39:9, 10)

These two poems have no direct relevance to the problem of theodicy, but they are a corrective to man's self-interest and his disregard for animal instincts. Job in his heyday was surrounded by servants (29:5) and his life-style required also the service of the vast herds of animals (1:1-3). These no longer serve him. His grievance against God is made with this background in mind (29-31) and to this extent the divine speech is a reply to the complaint of Job, and cannot be regarded as altogether irrelevant to the problematic of Job. One must admit, however, that nowhere in the divine speech is the Lord's care for man mentioned, and, of course, this was the one area on which Job criticised God. One can only hazard a guess that Job's high expectations of special privilege (e.g. 29:18, 19) are so much at variance with human experience that the very formulation of them on the lips of Job show them up for what they are – Utopian. Job is expecting too much from nature and from God. In Wisdom literature the most important truths may be unexpressed but nevertheless conveyed obliquely.

The Ostrich (39:13-18)

This poem is the strangest of all in the divine speech, in that it alone presents its subject in a totally unflattering light. Today we may laugh at the bird which is supposed to stick its head in the sand, but the Joban poem is far from being comic relief. The theme is the heartless cruelty of the ostrich to her own chicks – a totally unnatural trait. Students of natural history do not agree with the poet's assessment in this matter, but that need not concern us. It seems certain that the poet did not deliberately concoct a falsehood simply to buttress his case; the low opinion of the ostrich was widespread in the culture of his time (see Lam 4:3).

And the supposedly cruel way of the ostrich towards her young is attributed to God: 'For God denied her wisdom and left her without sense' (39:17).

The only other example in Job where God is accused of such harshness is in Job's own words:

> He (God) leads peoples astray and destroys them ... He takes away their wisdom from the rulers of the nations, and leaves them wandering in a pathless wilderness (12:23, 24).

In this passage, Job blames God for perverting justice in society by depriving the leaders (listed in 12:17-24) of their wisdom, and so bringing immense suffering on their subjects.

The ostrich and her helpless young is then a parallel to the leaders and their suffering subjects. The ostrich poem in the divine speech is a warning to Job that even in God's creation there are some serious imperfections, destructive and deadly tendencies deeply rooted in the nature of things.

In a veiled way the divine speech is agreeing to some extent with Job's pessimistic view of the world. For Job, in his despair, everything is hopeless; in the divine speech, while many things are wonderful and beneficial, there are some areas where evil triumphs.

One fact of experience which Job lamented was that the wicked go unpunished. The divine speech, while citing many mighty works of God, never claims explicitly that God puts down the wicked, and thus Job's claim seems to go unchallenged. One passage (38:13-15) which might seem to imply that God did throw down the wicked is capable of receiving a different translation, as in the NEB.

The cruelty of the ostrich to its own chicks may then be a pointer to human wickedness which has brought so much suffering to the innocent throughout the history of man, a wickedness that is deeply rooted in human nature, and which constitutes a continuing mystery of evil.

At the end of this depressing picture the poet, however, lets the ostrich display her one redeeming feature as she swiftly struts over the uplands, 'scorning both horse and rider' (39:18). A little bit of humour to lift the sadness?

The War-Horse (39:19-25)

Today we think of the horse in the context of agriculture and of sport, but in ancient times the horse had enormous importance in warfare, and the very existence of a nation might depend on its chariotry and its cavalry. Isaiah can speak of people who put their trust in horses rather than in Yahweh for national security, and the well-built stables at Megiddo still remind us that the Israelite monarchy invested heavily in its war-horses. At the battle of Qarqar (854BC) king Ahab of Israel took the field with 2,000 chariots against the Assyrians – a piece of information coming not from the Bible, where Ahab receives very unfavourable notice, but from Assyrian records.

Israelite archaeology has uncovered no artistic representation of the war-horse but this was not due to lack of familiarity with the same but rather on religious grounds. Egyptian art, however, had no such restrictions, and the magnificent paintings of Tutan-khamun in his chariot drawn by two festooned chargers are among the treasures of antiquity. Assyrian art also has notable examples. And so on right down to the great Pompeian mosaic of Alexander the Great on horseback at the Battle of Issus, and the eqyestrian stat-ue of Marcus Aurelius in Rome so admired by Michelangelo, whose reputed comment was spoken in praise of the horse rather than the rider.

And that is how it is with the poem in Job. It is the horse that gets all the praise, the rider isn't even mentioned. This passage on the war-horse is unique. It is the only artistic appreciation of the animal in the Bible. After touching briefly on the animal's strength, its flowing mane, its quivering skin, and shrill neighing, the poet con-centrates on the amazing courage of the animal as it eagerly charges the armoured line with all its might, and 'cannot be held in when he hears the horn, and at the blast of the horn he cries "Aha"' (29:24).

What is the function of this powerful poem in the context of the Book of Job? It certainly does not directly address the problem of why the innocent person suffers, but it does directly reply to Job's manner of presenting his case in chapter 29 where we have the most unusual poem of inflated self-esteem in the whole Bible. Job, speak-ing of his former life says:

> If I went through the gate out of the town
> to take my seat in the public square,
> young men saw me and kept out of sight;
> old men rose to their feet,
> men in authority broke off their talk
> and put their hands to their lips;
> the voice of the nobles died away,
> and everyman held his tongue.

> I presided over them, planning their course,
> like a king encamped with his troops (29:7-10; 25).

The divine speech, including the passage on the war-horse, is the answer to Job's self-esteem, and is a salutary reminder to him of the superiority of other creatures over man. The war-horse is superior to man in courage; Behemoth-Leviathan is superior to man in strength. Job used regal language for his own self-portrait (29:25), and the Lord uses the same language of Behemoth (40:19) and of Leviathan (41:33, 34). The passage on the war-horse is the answer to human hybris as manifested in Job's long speech in chapter 29.

For some commentators one of the disappointments of the divine speeches is their total refusal to deal with the problem of Job in the terms in which he and his friends had formulated it. Job himself had hoped and prayed in earnest and poignant words for a meeting with God and his heavenly court where Job's witness would testify in his favour and win his case. When eventually the Lord addresses Job out of the whirlwind there is no court case, and no witness to testify to Job's integrity. Moreover there is total silence on God's part on all the positions taken up by the three friends, and by the story of the Prologue. The list is formidable:

All the motifs listed below come from the lips of Job only, and are all brief moments of hope expressed in imagery of great power. They are all the impossible dreams of a despairing man who takes refuge in mythical fantasy. Each of the four passages consists of a few verses which are unrelated to their immediate contexts:

> *1) An Arbiter (9: 33-35):*
> If only there were an arbiter between us
> who would lay his hand on us both,
> who would take away God's club from me,
> so that my dread of him would not terrify me.
> Then I would speak without fear of him.

> *2) A Heavenly Witness (16:19-21):*
> Even now, in fact, my witness is in heaven,
> he who vouches for me is on high,
> interpreter of my thoughts to God,
> to whom my eye pours out its tears
> while he pleads for a man with God
> as a man does for a friend.

> *3) A Vindicator (Redeemer) (19:25-27):*
> For I know that my vindicator lives,
> and that at last he will stand upon the earth;

and after my skin has thus been thus destroyed
then in my flesh I shall see God,
whom I shall see for myself,
with my own eyes I shall behold him, not with another's.
My heart faints within me.

4) Temporary Refuge in The Underworld (14:13-15):
O that you would hide me in Sheol,
that you would conceal me until your anger is past
That you would appoint a set time and remember me.
All my weary days I would endure,
until my release should come.
You would call me, and I would answer you;
You would long for the work of your hands.

But in the divine speeches none of these hopes is realised:

1. No umpire or arbiter (9:33) who could decide the dispute between God and Job, and impose his authority over both of them. This impossible dream of Job fades away never to return after its brief appearance (9:33-35).[1]

2. No heavenly witness to speak in Job's favour (16:19) by virtue of his truthful testimony to Job's innocence. The heavenly court could then be expected to give Job a verdict of acquittal. But this hope fades away like the other after a brief moment (16:19-20).

3. No *go'ël* (vindicator, advocate, redeemer) stands up to defend Job (19:25). This hope, like the other two, consists only of three verses (19:25-27) and is not sustained in Job's later utterances, except in 31:35. See Text.

4. No temporary refuge for Job in She'ol until the divine wrath has passed over (14:13-15). Surely an original variation on the She'ol myth, with deep pathos and an appeal to the divine compassion; again only three verses of faint hope that stand out from their context, and are never taken up again.

But quite apart from these four passages there are four others which figure large in the earlier positions of the book and to which no reference whatever is made in the divine speeches:

5. No reference to the testing of Job – the whole story of the Prologue (chapters 1 and 2) which seeks to find an explanation of innocent suffering in the theory that God is testing Job.

6. No reference to the theory of retribution, proposed by the three friends, that Job's sufferings are due to his sins.

7. No confirmation of Job's own claim to be innocent comes in the divine speeches. Job hears no verdict of acquittal.

8. No reference, favourable or otherwise, of the view of Elihu that Job's sufferings may have a disciplinary value.

These four motifs, plus the earlier group of four, constitute between them a whole range of powerfully expressed and varied approaches to the debate on theodicy. How then explain the total silence of the Lord in the divine speeches on the relative merits of these various solutions, and his refusal to offer any alternative? Are the divine speeches, in spite of their beautiful poetry about earth and clouds and sea and wild animals and Leviathan, simply evading the problem, while, at the same time forcing the innocent Job to submit to the all-powerful God (42:1-6)? Is the poet using his considerable artistic skills (especially in the first speech) to cover up great theological weaknesses so as to support the edifice of his people's piety? I do not think so. But how then evaluate the divine speeches?

The divine speeches span the whole world known to man. All the vast array of earth and heavens, of wild life, of land and sky, of the waters of the deep and their dangerous monsters – all this is paraded before the eyes of Job – to what purpose?

If we follow an approach suggested by Karl Barth (*Church Dogmatics*) and taken up by G. von Rad (*Wisdom in Israel*, Eng. Tr. London, 1975, 225) that God, in the divine speeches allows creation to speak for him, without any special revelations of divine ways, then the mind of Job would be drawn to see God as powerful and orderly in his founding of the earth and heavens, and as benevolent in his providing for the animals of the wild who are not cared for by man. But this line of thought has its limitations. Job had never denied the power and knowledge of God. What he did deny was the justice of God in the moral governance of the world. And on this topic the divine speeches are silent. In fact the whole topic of the creation of man is never touched upon, while line after line describes the ostrich and the war-horse and finally Behemoth-Leviathan, monsters very dangerous for man, in which Job cannot discern the hand of a caring God. God is allowing some parts of creation to speak for him, but a notable part of creation, viz. man, has not been called to give evidence.

Perhaps a fruitful approach to the enigma of the divine speeches is to put the emphasis not on what it tells Job about the created world but on what it does *not* tell Job. True, Job is being shown the created world and its wonders, but he is also being invited to admit how little he understands the ways of the Creator. What Job is being asked in the divine speeches are questions touching God's counsel

(38:2) – his ways in creation and providence – cosmic wisdom, so to speak.[2]

'Were you there when I laid the foundations of the earth?' (38:4;NEB.) No, of course Job wasn't there. He was not an observer of cosmic wisdom at work in the orderly founding of the earth. The function of the rhetorical questions which dominate the divine speeches is primarily negative: to emphasise that Job does not know God's cosmic ways.[3] The divine speeches do not tell Job anything he doesn't already know. He is given no 'behind the scenes' view of God's creative work. It is not the case that God is withholding information from Job. It's simply that God's design is too wonderful for Job's comprehension: 'Things too wonderful for me' (42 3d; cf 9:10).

In this respect we may note the difference between the Egyptian letter (thirteenth century BC) of the official Hori to the scribe Amenem-Opet, who is chided for not knowing 'what the city of Byblos is like, and its goddess? Once again thou hast not trodden it'. The scribe cannot speak about Beirut, Sidon and Sarepta, and doesn't know where the Litani river is (See J. B. Pritchard, *Ancient Near Eastern Texts*, 2 ed, Princeton, 1955 [Abbreviated*ANET*], p 477). But he should know these and many other such things, as a responsible government official. Job on the contrary could not be expected to know the cosmic secrets of God – he is not chided for his lack of knowledge of such deep matters, but he is reminded that his lack of knowledge of God's ways excludes him from passing judgment on God's governance of the world. The divine speeches are ultimately educating Job and leading him to the truth about God's transcendence (42:5), and Job feels he knows God better as a result: 'Now my eye has seen thee' (42:5b), whereas the Hori letter merely serves to humiliate its recipient.

'Were you there when I laid the foundations of the earth?' (38:4)
This question from the first Divine Speech introduces a series of the most probing questions[4] in the whole Bible on the myth-making business of the ancient world: if Job (indeed, if any man) has not been present at creation, how can he make stories purporting to portray, in vivid imagery, what happened, and who were the participating agents? God's ways in creation and providence are hidden from Job, and Job's mistake was to darken God's counsel with words without knowledge (39:2), not that God's counsel, in itself, could be affected by any words of Job, but Job's theologising about it with his friends is what is intended. Job wasn't privy to God's

counsel. He is not the Primal Man – a heavenly figure originating from God before the ordering of the world, and thus having cosmic wisdom. Even though it is Yahweh who introduces the myth of the Primal Man into the divine speeches (39:21, but *cf* also 15:7,8) he does so only to exclude its application to Job. Whether the poet of Job thought there ever was such a Primal Man is not clear. Quite possibly he regarded the Primal Man as a myth of dubious origin (*cf* Isaiah 40:13,14), just another 'word without knowledge'.

If then the Lord, in the divine speeches, is moving Job's thoughts away from the whole mythological way of thinking about God's cosmic counsel, why does he introduce Behemoth and especially the mythical Leviathan at such great length?

The plural form Behemoth ('The Beast') occurs some half a dozen times in the Old Testament, always without mythical implications, but Leviathan is a well known mythical monster of chaos both in the Old Testament (including Job 3:8) and in other Ancient Near Eastern literature (in Ugaritic myth as Lotan). But the passage in the divine speeches when Leviathan is introduced, 41:1 (Hb 40:25) mentions none of the features which would clearly identify it as the great many-headed dragon of chaos who fought with God at creation. The Leviathan of chapter 41 constitutes a threat not to God but to man. It may well be that the mythical term is being used merely as a metaphor for the crocodile with its great strength and agility, which made it an object of fear and wonder even for the Egyptians who were more familiar with it.[5] Thus in the Hymn of Victory of Thut–mose III (1490-1436) the following words are spoken by Amon-Re to the Pharaoh:

> The lands of Mitanni are trembling under the fear of thee
> I cause them to see thy majesty as a crocodile,
> The Lord of fear in the water, who cannot be approached–
> (*ANET*, p 373)

From all this, I think we may conclude that while mythical names like Leviathan may continue to be used in their full mythical impact in Job 3:8 (*cf* also 9:13 for Rehab) and in creation poems like Ps 74:13f, the same names may also be applied metaphorically to non-mythical subjects like Job himself (7:12) or the Pharaoh (Ezek 29:3), or the crocodile.

A further and novel suggestion is to interpret the Leviathan of Job 41:1-6, not as introducing a new subject distinct from Behemoth but simply as referring back to Behemoth (40:15), under a new title, just as Job himself used *tannin* (7:12) to refer to himself, and just as Ezekiel in 29:3 used Leviathan to refer back to the Pharaoh.

The New English Bible interprets Behemoth (40:15) as the crocodile, rather than the hippopotamus as many others do. Although
there are difficulties in the NEB approach, as indeed in other interpretations, I propose to follow its lead in seeing the crocodile as the
creature referred to. Yahweh, who had spoken of the land animals
and of the birds of the air, now very appropriately finishes with the
greatest representative of the aquatic world – the crocodile, 'the
chief of God's ways' (40:19). This creature is not mythical, it is real.
It constitutes a threat not to God but to the man who would try to
dominate it:

> 'Can one take him with hooks or pierce his nose with a
> snare?' (40:24)
> 'Can you draw out Leviathan with a fishhook, or press down
> his tongue with a cord?' (Hb 40:25)

One can see that 40:24, in spite of the poor state of textual preser-
vation, has already begun the theme of the invincible nature of the
creature, a theme continued for the next several verses. The term
Leviathan introduced in the next verse (Hb 40:25; RSV 41:1) is commonly taken as introducing a second monster distinct from
Behemoth, but this may not be necessary, as we saw. 'Leviathan'
here may be used metaphorically of Behemoth, to emphasise its
magnificent strength and agility as an opponent of the man foolish
enough to try to dominate it. There is never any reference in chapter
41 to Leviathan's many heads nor to his having been vanquished by
God at creation or after. And it's not as if our poet were pressed for
space to say these things. All the various techniques of the fisher-
man trying to land a crocodile are explored and this should tilt the
balance away from interpreting the Leviathan of chapter 41 in a
strictly mythical way. The world to which the Lord is drawing Job's
attention in all the divine speeches is the world of the earth, sky,
land and water, the real world of human experience and of human
wonder and the last and finest of these wonders of God's creation
described is Behemoth–Leviathan.

Although the divine speeches present a vast panorama of creation, there is surely one strange omission: man. Has the Lord not
remembered his crowning act of creation (Ps 8)? Another serious
omission is that, while God's knowledge and power are celebrated,
there is silence on God's justice, specifically with regard to man and
his sufferings. Job had no need to be informed on God's knowledge
and power (9:4ff), but had questioned divine justice in a most daring way. Here again a blank silence. There is nothing at all in the
divine speeches about God's restoration of the afflicted, nor about

all the tender works of mercy which one looks for in a good man, not to mention a good God.

Job himself, in former days, had delivered the poor who cried, and the fatherless who had none to help him (29:12). But now, in his sufferings, when he turns to God for help, he receives none.

He complains to God:

'I cry to you and you do not answer me' (30:20).

'Did not I weep for him whose day was hard? Was not my soul grieved for the poor? But when I looked for good evil came' (30:25).

Moreover, the Lord never sets up a heavenly court in which Job's witness, umpire, or *go'ĕl* could speak the truth in Job's favour. And the Lord never even hints to Job that he sees Job as an innocent man, or that he was only being tested all the time, as the Prologue had stated.

There are so many silences in the divine speech that we must try to fathom its credibility as a worthy conclusion to a great poem. To help us in this quest, the poet himself, I suggest, supplies us with three useful guidelines.

There are, I think, three guiding principles which the poet-theologian has forcefully proposed within the poetry sections of Job, and which he adheres to in his composition of the divine speeches. The first two are placed on the lips of Job himself, and the third is in the famous Wisdom poem, chapter 28.

The first is the precedence of observation and critical reflection over tradition. Job, in this, joins the powerful thrust of the international Wisdom movement in the post-exilic centuries, with its emphasis on observation and reflection.

Bildad had advised Job to listen to tradition, i.e. to the voice of the older generations whose accumulated experience was more weighty than the limited insights of the present generation (8:8-16). The voice of the fathers would inform Job that wickedness always brought down the wrath of God. Job, however, would not accept this. In a strange and unusual penetration of the depths of animal consciousness, he tells his listener to ask the cattle, the birds of the air, and creatures that crawl if they do not experience the enigma of God's ways when great natural catastrophes suddenly strike them down without cause (12:9). Secondly Job's friends ought to listen to the observations of travellers who bring home their testimony to the great mockery of justice evidenced in the splendid funeral given to an evil tyrant who was never punished for his sins (12:29-34). Thirdly, Job's own observation and experience of the triumph of

evil and chaos in the world (12:13-22) is the firm ground on which
he takes his stand:

> 'All this I have seen with my own eyes, with my own ears I
> have heard it, and understand it'.

Job's own experience, and that of others who have travelled, and
even of the animals, in all these cases the experience concerns the
overthrow of justice. Finally, Job testifies to the state of his own conscience (27:6). This is moral observation of the subject by the subject, and has received, on the lips of Job, the fullest attestation in two
memorable chapters of his final soliloquy (29, 31).

There are, in fact, in the divine speeches, only two faults for
which the Lord reproaches Job: one that in defending his own
moral integrity he had condemned the Lord (40:8), and two, that he
had ignored the complexity and enormous range of God's mysteri-
ous ways in creation and so had obscured God's design with 'words
without knowledge' (38:2). Job is nowhere required to retract his
protestations of innocence nor his observation of the triumph of evil
in the real world of men. The three friends, relying on the traditional
dogma of divine retribution, had required Job to confess to some
hidden fault, but Job stoutly placed the testimony of his conscience
above the force of tradition. And the divine speeches did not
reproach him for this, nor for any sin to which his sufferings might
be attributed.

It seems then that the principle of the precedence of experience
and reflection over tradition, which the poet had placed on the lips
of Job, is maintained by the poet as a guideline in the composition
of the divine speeches.

The second principle concerns the primacy of truthfulness in
theological debate. Job is aware that the purpose of the widely held
retribution principle is to uphold God's just governance of the
world in rewarding the good and punishing the wicked. His friends
have interpreted Job's calamity as divine punishment for his sins.
Job refuses to accept their interpretation, and by insisting that his
conscience is free of serious sin, calls into question the widely
accepted theodicy. He is acutely aware of the dilemma himself, but
he insists on giving priority to his conscience at the expense of their
theodicy, and also he accuses the friends of going against their sure
knowledge of his good character simply in order to maintain theologically respectable dogma. His principle then is that truthfulness
must never be sacrificed in one's defence of God. He goes further
and states that God will punish the friends for violating this principle. God does not wish to be defended with men's lies and Job says
to his friends:

'Will you speak falsely for God and speak deceitfully for him? Will you show partiality towards him and will you plead the case for God? Will it be well with you when he searches you out? He will surely rebuke you if in secret you show partiality' (13:7-10).

It is always the desire of devout souls to defend God's honour in religious debate, but the temptation sometimes presents itself to be less than honest when faced with serious objections that seem to threaten the edifice of theodicy. To such a temptation the friends have succumbed. Job tells them: 'You, like fools, are smearing truth with your falsehoods' (1 3:4) – doing a cosmetic job, so to speak, to save God's face, as they see it, by inventing lies.

For Job, however, the primary duty is to witness to the truth in spite of unpleasant consequences:

'… I will speak, and let come on me what may' (13:13).

'Behold, he (God) will slay me; I have no hope; Yet I will defend my ways to his face' (13: 15).

It is remarkable that in the divine speeches Job is never asked to speak against his conscience. He is never told that his sufferings were caused by any sins he had committed. The poet who made Job talk so boldly about the priority of truthfulness over traditional theodicy, is not going to go back on this when he composes the divine reply. God respects the conscience of Job. The poet of the divine speeches may sometimes be chided for taking us on a wild goose chase all over the cosmos, and exhibiting the bizarre and the irrelevant like the silly ostrich and the horse who cries 'Aha', and saying nothing about the innocent sufferer Job who is sitting in front of him, but that poet can never be accused of covering up the cracks of a broken theodicy. He would prefer to leave the problem unsolved than to pretend he had settled it. The passion for truth, for finding truth and holding it, has taken possession of the author, and he will not let go. On the matter of theodicy, our poet's position is that Job's only fault was not that he maintained his own integrity, but that in so doing he denied God's integrity (40:8). For this latter he is rebuked, but not for the former.

The third principle which seems to influence our poet in his approach to the composition of the divine speeches derives from his lack of sympathy with mythopoeic thinking. The brand of Wisdom which he espouses, in contrast to that of Sirach and others, emphasised the importance not only of keen observation, but also of intellectual reflection on what was observed, and technological exploration of the earth. This reliance on what man can observe and control inevitably diminished his interest in the whole range of ancient thought connected with priesthood, ritual, myth, and prophetic oracles as guides to living and thinking. It is remarkable, for instance, that in Job's great confession of innocence (in chapter 31) in the long list of his honourable deeds there is no reference to his fulfilment of any positive ritual precept, whereas in the older Egyptian counterpart – the confession before Osiris – ritual performances (as well as moral conduct) figure. In the divine speeches there are no references to ritual, to priesthood, or to prophetic oracles. So, once again we find a correspondence of outlook between Job at his most sublime (chapter 31) and the divine speeches. In both instances the poet, in lines of sustained power and depth, is revealing the structures of his own theological thinking.

The importance of technology in the Wisdom movement is exemplified in the great poem of 28:1-11. These eleven verses are really the finest celebration of man's exploratory prowess in mining for precious ores, finding his way into the dark secrets of the earth, and sinking shafts into the roots of the mountains. Technology is the sphere of man's greatest control of the earth for his own purposes. But when man leaves this area of his high achievement, and seeks the way to the higher, invisible wisdom of the cosmos, he cannot find it. As a later sage admitted, 'even though a wise man may claim to know, he cannot find it out' (Ecc 8:17). So the second part of the Wisdom poem (28:12-22) admits that such wisdom is distant and hidden from man and beyond the range of his skills. God alone understands the way to it (28:23), and, in the book of Job at any rate, does not reveal it to man.

The search for cosmic wisdom is futile, and man does well to concentrate his energies where they bear most fruit – in observation of nature, reflection and the development of technology. The great achievements in engineering under Hezekiah, by which the Siloam tunnel was successfully completed, brought the waters of the spring Gihon from outside the walls of Jerusalem, under the walls of the city into the Siloam reservoir. This amazing feat of technology, which enabled Jerusalem to withstand the Assyrian invasion (701BC), is commemorated for all time in the Siloam inscription. In its six lines of finely cursive Hebrew script, this plaque to the technological spirit mentions neither God nor king, but is totally devoted to 'the matter of the tunnelling' through the final four and a half feet of rock which was being excavated from both sides. It ends with precise measurements of the length and height of the tunnel. And to store this water within the city another feat of technology – the discovery of waterproof lime mortar – made the construction of the reservoir possible (Is 22:11).

But these achievements in technology could bring dangers to the faith in their train. Isaiah, who refers to the reliance on technology for national security, senses the danger that the nation is no longer relying on ('looking to') God (Is 22:8-11). This wisdom mentality tended to be autonomous, and Isaiah found that the statecraft of the wise counsellors of the king in Jerusalem was not receptive to the prophetic word, nor to Israel's *Tora*. Statecraft was an international discipline in which a highly educated elite could attain to an intellectual grasp of human affairs and explore ways of resolving international tensions by diplomacy or, failing that, through the arduous ways of warfare, when technology was of supreme importance.

This mentality – positivist, pragmatic, scientific – is not the natural soil for mythological thinking. And while the poet of Job may, in the divine speeches, borrow some mythical allusions from the common fund of ancient poetic imagery, he does so sparingly, just to add a touch of colour or embellishment to his thought. But fully mythical narratives like the Prologue draw no response from him, because they are too remote from his observations of nature and of man's world. He does, of course, believe in God, and professes to see something of the Creator's power and wisdom, reflected in the mighty and complex works of nature. But this 'something' is very little – indeed only 'the fringe of his domain', only a faint 'whisper' (if this is how the rare word *sms* in 26:14 is to be translated).

The divine speeches do not answer Job in the terms in which Job had formulated his requests. But these terms were cast in the mythological imagery of the heavenly court at which Job's case would be upheld by an umpire, or a witness, or *go'el*. In the divine speeches our poet refuses to resort to myths to solve the real problems of human suffering, and he is too passionately truthful to fake a solution. For him a happy ending in terms of a mythical trial in which Job would be vindicated before a celestial assembly would offer no solace to the innocent sufferers of the real world who have to suffer on in the dark without experiencing any such celestial comforts in the earthly existence.

If this is the case, why then did the same poet who, in the divine speeches, refuses a mythical solution, himself introduce the mythical element in Job's hopes for a heavenly witness etc? There are quite special features about the first four mythological hopes of Job: they are found only on the lips of Job; they are quite brief, only a few verses each; they form no connection with the drift of argument before or after them. In each case Job rises above his deep despair for a few poignant moments of impossible hope, only to sink back again into the ocean of his sorrow. The difficulties which commentators experience in interpreting the deeply emotional *go ʾel* passage are not all due to textual corruption. The poet is being deliberately enigmatic because he knows he is describing the 'utterances of a despairing man' (6:26), whose heart is fainting within him (19:27). In such extreme distress of mind, Job has for a fleeting moment reached out for mythical solutions. But the poet, by the manner in which he suddenly introduces them and then abruptly terminates them, leaving his readers puzzled, is indicating that these mythical solutions do not offer a real solution to Job's plight, and so they do not find any response in the divine reply to Job (38-41).

It would seem then that the divine silence on the many issues raised by Job and his friends is not due to the poet's inability or unwillingness to face the difficult problems of theodicy. It is due to his refusal to answer the problems in the terms in which they were presented. And these terms were, as we might say, mythological, or, as the poet himself might say, in 'words without knowledge', in imagery of heavenly assemblies or courts of law where celestial witnesses etc. made their appearance, or in the presumption that man could probe into the complexity of the divine mind. But some of the later Wisdom thinkers, like Qoheleth and the poet of Job, acknowledged that such cosmic wisdom was beyond the range of man's real competence, and they refused to debate theological problems in such mythical terms. The mind that seeks the truth as passionately as Job will not settle for a *refugium in fabulas*. The poet of Job may well have felt that while the high point of his poem's emotion and pathos is reached in the long soliloquy of Job (29-31), the high point of theological reflection is in the divine speeches, in the intellectual honesty with which the problem is there faced, and the limitations of human knowledge are admitted, and God's mystery and transcendence are acknowledged.

But the long poem of Job does not conclude on the disappointing note that Job is left without any light on his problem. It is not quite true to say that Job, after listening to the divine speeches, is no wiser than he was before. Job, in his own final reply (42:1-6) admits that he now appreciates God's transcendence better than before, and that he now sees that God's design is too complex for the human mind to judge it's performance, and that therefore Job's accusations against God were 'words without knowledge'. And this is a gain for Job. Moreover, Job has not been asked to speak against his conscience, he has not been forced to deny his own innocence. He is left with the mystery of suffering but he no longer feels obliged to interpret this as God's injustice towards him. And for a deeply religious man like Job this is a consolation.

> 'I had heard of thee by the hearing of the ear, but now my eyes see thee' (42:5).

Job, in the end, finds reconcilement not with the God of the myths, but with the God of mystery. He accepts nature in all its wondrous and dangerous forces, on the earth, in the sky, and in the waters, as showing forth the Lord of the cosmos.

Notes:

1. Such an arbiter is superior in authority to both parties in the dispute. The suggestions that the umpire may be one of the heavenly council or a personal God on the model of the Sumerian personal god, who could appeal to the great gods, fail to recognise this superiority of the arbiter who can 'lay his hand on both of us' (9:33). Job knows of no being so great as to lay his hand on the Almighty. Even the goddess Ningal failed to exercise any influence over the great gods An and Enlil when they decreed the destruction of Ur. When they turned down her appeal she came before the solemn session of the gods and repeated her plea, but in vain. See 'Lamentation over the Destruction of Ur', J. B. Pritchard, *Ancient Near Eastern Texts*, Princeton, 1955, p 458.

2. The wisdom movement in Israel, as in the wider world of the Ancient Near East, had two distinct aspects to it: while it stored up traditional wisdom in well-polished proverbs, guidelines for practical affairs of the home and of the court, it had also attempted to face the larger and more philosophical problems of the meaning of life and of the great cosmos of which man was part. Wisdom could be of two kinds: practical or cosmic. Job is searching for cosmic wisdom – but he cannot find it (*cf* chap 28).

3. The force of 38:21 'You know, for you were born then ...' is clearly ironic.

4. In chapters 38 and 39 the poet combines questions on the twin motifs of Job's lack of knowledge of the mysteries of creation, and his lack of power to perform the works of God. These two motifs are intertwined: 10 verses on the lack of knowledge (38:2-11) followed by 4 on the lack of power (38:2-15), then 18 on the lack of knowledge followed by 7 on the lack of power, and so on, with an overall ratio of 2 (knowledge): 1 (power). This combination ends with chapter 39. From chapter 40 on, all the questions concern Job's impotence in face of the dangerous Behemoth-Leviathan. Man's dominion over nature is not complete. There are dark forces in nature hostile to him. The optimistic picture of Genesis 1 needs qualification.

5. This metaphorical use of a mythical term can be seen in Ezek 29:3. 'Behold, I will come over you, Pharaoh, King of Egypt, the great dragon, that lies in the midst of the currents of the river.' Job himself had already used such a term metaphorically in 7:12:

'Am I a sea (*yam*), or a sea-monster (*tannin*)
That you set a guard over me?'

If the poet of Job wishes to speak in creation myths of the primordial conflict between God and his enemies (Yam and Rehab) he is well able to do
so, as in 26:12, but in the whole long poem on Behemoth-Leviathan there is
nothing of all this primordial conflict. The only conflict is between man and
Behemoth-Leviathan, and then only if man tries to dominate the strong
Beast. In fact the Lord is rather proud of his mighty creature and is lauding
his fine qualities like a farmer parading his prize bull at a show. *Cf* also Is
27:1 for the metaphorical use of the term Leviathan.

Summary: The divine speeches
Chapters 38-41

Both speeches were spoken 'out of the whirlwind', the frightening and destructive forces of nature (which had killed Job's children, 1:19).

In the Lord's first speech (38:1-39:30) he challenges Job to stand up like a man and answer questions which are designed to teach Job how ill-informed his condemnation of the Lord had been. Job is presented with a whole panorama of the wonders of the cosmos, of the strange habits and instincts of wild animals. Job's criticisms had been 'words without knowledge' (38:2).

Job replies that he feels overwhelmed by the wisdom of his mighty opponent, and opts for silence (40:4,5).

In the Lord's second speech (40:6-41:26) come the dangerous water monsters, Behemoth and Leviathan, masterpieces of God's power.

Job's reply (42:1-6) is to acknowledge the Lord's wisdom and power, and to admit he had spoken 'of things beyond my understanding' (42:3), but that 'Now I see', I know God better now than I did formerly.

Text: The divine speeches

38: 1 And the Lord answered Job out of the whirlwind and said:
2 Who is this that obscures my design by words without
       knowledge?
3 Gird up your loins like a man,
   I will question you, and you shall answer me.
4 Where were you when I laid the foundations of the earth?
   Tell me, if you have insight!
5 Who determined the measures thereof? for surely you know.
   And who stretched the measuring-line upon it?
6 Upon what were its pillar-sockets set?
   And who laid its corner-stone,
7 When the morning stars sang together,
   And all the sons of God shouted for joy?

8 Who shut in the sea with doors,
   When it burst forth, issuing from the womb?
9 When I made the clouds its garment,
   And the dark cloud its swaddling clothes,
10 And prescribed bounds for it,
   And set bars and doors,
11 And said: Thus far shall you come, and no farther,
   And here shall your proud waves be turned back.

12 Have you ordered the morning since your days began?
   Have you shown the dawn its place,
13 That it might take hold of the ends of the earth,
   And that the wicked be shaken out of it?
14 So that it is changed like clay under the seal,
   And is dyed like a garment;
15 And from the wicked their light is withdrawn,
   And the uplifted arm is broken.

33 Do you know the ordinances that govern the heavens?
    Can you establish their rule on the earth?

The Lioness

38: 39 Can you hunt the prey for the lioness?
         Can you satisfy the appetite of the lion-cubs?
     40 When they crouch in their dens,
         And abide in their lairs?
     41 Who provides for the raven his food
         …
         When his young cry unto God,
         And wander about without food?

The Mountain Goats

39:   1 'Do you know when the mountain goats give birth?
         Do you observe the calving of the deer?
      2 Can you number the months that they fulfil,
         and do you know the time when they give birth,
      3 when they crouch to give birth to their offspring,
         and are delivered of their young?
      4 Their young ones become strong, they grow up in the open;
         they go forth, and do not return to them.

The Wild Ass

      5 Who has let the wild ass go free?
         And who has loosed the bonds of the wild ass? –
      6 Whose home I have made the wilderness,
         And whose dwelling-place the salt land?
      7 He scorns the tumult of the city,
         And hears not the shouts of the driver;
      8 He explores the mountains, his pasture,
         He seeks after every green thing.

The Wild Ox

      9 Will the wild ox consent to serve you?
         Will he spend the night at your manger?
     10 Will you bind him with a halter of cord?
         Will he harrow the valleys after you?
     11 Will you trust in him because his strength is great?
         And will you entrust your labour to him?
     12 Will you rely on him to return?
         Will he gather your grain to your threshing-floor?

The Ostrich

13 The ostrich's wings flap wildly,
   though its pinions lack plumage.

14 For it leaves its eggs to the earth,
   And lets them be warmed on the ground,

15 Forgetting that a foot may crush them,
   and that a wild animal may trample them.

16 It deals cruelly with its young,
   As if they were not its own;
   Though its labour should be in vain,
   Yet it has no fear;

17 Because God has made it forget wisdom,
   And given it no share in understanding.

18 When it spreads its plumes aloft,
   It laughs at the horse and its rider.

The War-Horse

19 Do you give the horse his might?
   Do you clothe his neck with a quivering mane?

20 Do you make him leap like a locust?
   The glory of his snorting is terrible,

21 He paws in the valley and exults;
   In his strength he goes forth to meet weapons,

22 He laughs at fear, and is not dismayed,
   And turns not back from the sword;

23 The quiver rattles against him,
   The flashing point of lance and javelin,

24 Quivering and excited he swallows the ground;
   He cannot stand still at the sound of the trumpet.

25 When the trumpet sounds, he says 'Aha!'
   From a distance he smells the battle,
   The thunder of the captains, and the shouting.

The Hawk

26 Is it by your wisdom that the hawk soars,
   That he spreads his wings toward the south?

27 Is it at your behest that the vulture goes aloft,
   And makes his nest on high?

28 On the crag he dwells and abides,
   On the peak of the crag and the fastness;

29 From thence he spies out the prey,
   His eyes look into the far distance;

30 His young ones suck up the blood,
And where the slain are, there is he.

The Lord's Challenge
40:    1 And the Lord said to Job:
2 'Shall a faultfinder contend with the Almighty?
Anyone who argues with God must respond.'

Job's Response
3 Then Job answered the Lord:
4 'See, I am of small account; what shall I answer you?
I lay my hand on my mouth.
5 I have spoken once, and I will not answer;
twice, but will do so no more.

The Lord's Second Speech
6 Then the Lord answered Job out of the whirlwind:
7 'Gird up your loins like a man;
I will question you, and you declare to me.
8 Will you even put me in the wrong?
Will you condemn me that you may be justified?
9 Have you an arm like God,
and can you thunder with a voice like his?
10 Deck yourself with majesty and dignity;
clothe yourself with glory and splendour.
11 Pour out the overflowings of your anger,
And look on all who are proud, and abase them.
12 Look on all who are proud, and bring them low;
Tread down the wicked where they stand.
13 Hide them all in the dust together;
Bind their faces in the world below.
14 Then I will also acknowledge to you
That your own right hand can give you victory.

The Monster Behemoth-Leviathan
15 'Look at Behemoth, which I made just as I made you;
It eats grass like an ox.
16 Its strength is in its loins,
And its power in the muscles of its belly.
17 It makes its tail stiff like a cedar;
The sinews of its thighs are knit together.

18 Its bones are tubes of bronze,
    Its limbs like bars of iron.
19 It is the first of the great works of God
    …

23 Even if the river is turbulent, it is not frightened;
    it is confident, even though the Jordan is in flood.
24 Can one take it in its lair,
    Or pierce its nose with a snare?
25 Can you draw out Leviathan with a fish-hook,
    Or press down its tongue with a line? ˙
26 Can you pass a cord through its nose,
    Or pierce its jaw with a hook?
27 Will it plead with you for mercy,
    Or will it speak tender words to you?
    …

32 Lay your hand upon it;
    Think of the battle you'll have – you won't do it again
    …

41:     25 There is nothing like it upon the earth,
            A creature without fear,
        26 It surveys everyone that is lofty,
            It is king over all proud beasts.

Job's Final Reply to God

42:     1 Then Job answered the Lord:
        2 I know that you can do all things,
           and that no purpose of yours can be thwarted.
        3 'Who is this that darkens my design
           by words without knowledge?'
           Therefore I have uttered what I did not understand,
           things too wonderful for me, which I did not know.
        4 'Hear, and I will speak;
           I will question you, and you declare to me.'
        5 I had heard of you by the hearing of the ear,
           but now my eyes sees you;

Conclusion

        6 Therefore I *despise* (my words)
           and *repent* in dust and ashes.'

Or

        6 Therefore I *melt away*,
           and *am comforted* in dust and ashes.

Note on 42:6:

a) In the first line (42:6a) the Hebrew verb *ma'as* is usually regarded as a transitive verb: 'I despise' something or other. But in 42:6 no direct object is expressed, so translators supply either 'myself' or, (as I have done) 'my words'. But the verb *ma'as* may also possibly be taken as an intransitive form, giving a meaning like 'I pine away', 'I melt away' (in ecstasy, in anguish etc).

b) In the second line (42:6b) the verb used by Job is *nḥm*, sometimes translated 'I repent' (of my rash words against God), or 'I am comforted' (because I now know God better than before, 42:5).

Is the author thereby graciously inviting the reader to determine the final sentiments of Job with which his great poem ends? Is it repentance? – or is it consolation?

CHAPTER 5

Theodicy in the whirlwind

'Tempted to pray'

On 11 April 1987 the distinguished writer Primo Levi put a sudden end to his life by throwing himself down the stairwell of the apartment in Turin where he lived. That day was his *Dies Irae*, his day of wrath and sorrow, a day when he was overcome by personal distress, ill-health and depression. It was the sudden collapse of a man who forty years earlier had survived the humiliation and cruelty of the death camps in Auschwitz.

When he had emerged from Auschwitz after being liberated by the Russians he felt as in a coma, totally lost, for some months, until he found a purpose for living in writing about the camps. In his final book (*I Sommersi e I Salvati*, Turin, 1986, the year before his death), one feels he had said his final word on the gigantic evil that had blotted out all reason and civilisation, all justice and mercy from his world; he had tried to look beneath the terrible facts to the underlying motivation of the brutality, and, having revealed something of the moral sickness of man, the author had nothing further to add to the bleak picture. He fell back again into his spiritual coma, he was lost, and had no further reason for existence. He was an unbeliever – firmly and reflectively – and that fact also left him without hope. Was he, in his final year, even 'tempted to pray' ?

This question I leave unanswered; but the phrase 'tempted to pray' arises from a very moving passage in his last book. It tells of a terrible day in October 1944 when he came very close to death, and then, for the first and last time, he felt a need to pray for deliverance:

> I was waiting to file past the 'commission' that with one glance would decide whether I should immediately go into the gas chamber or was instead strong enough to go on working. For one instant I felt the need to ask for help and asylum. A prayer under these conditions would not only have been absurd (what rights could I claim? and from whom?) but blasphemous, obscene ....'[1]

The words in brackets deserve close scrutiny. It's true that if one really doesn't believe in God at all, then prayer in the sense of calling on God for help is absurd. But what about the other question 'what rights could I claim?' The language is clearly forensic and implies a concept of 'prayer' in which the emphasis is on what is due in justice to the petitioner rather than on the mercy and love of the Giver, and it also gives a clue to the author's idea of the God of his unbelief.

What kind of God does the author reject? He tells us that he entered the camp an unbeliever, and he left it an unbeliever, and thus remained 'until today'. The experience of the frightening iniquity of the camp only strengthened his unbelief (p 117). As he puts it: 'It has prevented me, and still prevents me, from conceiving any kind of providence or of transcendent justice' – a statement once again followed by two questions – this time without brackets and, in the original, without verbs: 'Why the moribund in cattle trucks? Why the children in gas?' Language terse, ultimate.

If one expects God to pluck the innocent victim out of the jaws of the wicked (to use Job's imagery), and this does not happen, then, either God does not exist, or if he does, he is totally different from what one thought. The only use of the term *providence* in the Hebrew Bible occurs in Job 10:12, and the image of God as a kind father, caring for the bodily well-being of his child, is spelt out – only to be rejected by Job, who, speaking from experience, denies God's intervention on behalf of the innocent sufferer.

Perhaps at this stage it is well to look at another Auschwitz prisoner, this time one who did not survive. He, unlike Levi, was a believer on entering the camp, and remained a believer to the end. For Maximilian Kolbe, Auschwitz was the place of his spiritual growth to the greatest love, love for God and love for his enemies who tortured him to death, and love for a young father of a family for whom Kolbe substituted himself in the death-cell.

In the last weeks of his life in Auschwitz, Maximilian saw no hope of survival for himself. Still his prayer-life intensified and brought spiritual comfort to many other prisoners. Prayers for deliverance, deliverance not from death which now was close at hand, but deliverance from hatred. Prayer also for God's consoling presence in the midst of sorrows. As Bruno Borgowiecs testified in his eye-witness account: 'From their cell each day came sounds of prayers being said aloud, the Rosary being recited, hymns being sung. The prisoners in the other cells joined in ... Sometimes they were so deep in prayer that they didn't hear the guards coming ....'[2]

And 'if we die, we die in holiness and peace, resigned to the will of God'.[3] Maximilian regarded his ministry to the inmates of the camp as an act of divine providence; it was his privilege to minister to the most forsaken of all God's creatures.

Here then we have two contrasting pictures from Auschwitz: one an unbeliever, the other a devoutly religious man.

In both cases, however, there was no deliverance from the physical sufferings and humiliation of the camp. God did not directly intervene to stop the brutality, and this very fact confirmed the unbelief of Levi, but did not undermine the faith of Kolbe. I cannot say it confirmed the faith of Kolbe, but it did not weaken it, and it gave scope for spiritual growth, love for God and love for others. God's providence, in Kolbe's view, was at work in Auschwitz, not in material ways, but in spiritual ways.

If we turn our gaze away from Central Europe to the camps in Russia, we see another host of the witnesses of human sorrow. The barbarism of our present century is so vast that one may feel the need of some comic relief. And, from the midst of the tears, 'the tears of the oppressed' of which Qohelet the poet spoke, there comes one of the most touching theological debates between Ivan Denisovich and the devout Alyosha, both prisoners.[4]

Ivan had had a 'good' day in the camp and had retired to bed and recited his farewell to the parting day with his usual: 'Glory to thee, O Lord. Another day over.' Alyosha overheard this brief antiphon, and turning to Ivan said: 'There you are, Ivan Denisovich, your soul is begging to pray. Why don't you give it its freedom?' But Ivan resisted the temptation to pray, and he had his reasons: 'However much you pray it won't shorten your stretch.' Alyosha, however, is not without an answer: 'O you musn't pray for that either. Why do you want freedom? In freedom your last grain of faith will be choked with weeds ... We must pray about things of the spirit – that the Lord Jesus should remove the scum of anger from our hearts.'

What emerges from the literature of captivity is that those who experienced the camps in which millions suffered and died saw no evidence of 'transcendent justice' (Levi's words), but some of the inmates who were believers, particularly those of strong religious or political faith (e.g. in Marx), continued to believe. Even Levi admits that the believers whom he knew in the camp 'all held in common the saving force of their faith. Their universe was vaster than ours (i.e. unbelievers). They had a millennial tomorrow, so that there might be a sense of sacrificing themselves, a place in heaven or on earth where justice and compassion had won.' 'Not only during the crucial moments of the selection or the aerial bombings, but also in the grind of everyday life, the believers lived better: both of us, Améry and I, observed this.' (p 118).

The thought that, even if the Lord does not snatch the innocent victim from the jaws of the persecutor, the believer can still feel close to God is also reflected in a convict song which Dostoyevsky recalls in his account of Russian prisons in his *House of the Dead*:

No one sees us in our prison,
How we live, together tossed;
God our Heavenly Creator's with us,
Even here we are not lost.[5]

Many Jews, like Primo Levi, and many Christians too, when they came to the camps, brought with them the image of God as the Saviour of his people in the great moments of Israel's history, and when they experienced nothing like this taking place in their own crises, they must have been tempted to conclude that there was no God. Speaking of his own youth he says 'We gathered in the School of the (Mosaic) Law - and taught each other to find again in the Bible justice and injustice and the strength that overcame injustice.'[6] Then comes the crucial question: 'But where was Kadosh Baruk hu (The Holy One, Blessed be he): he who breaks the slave's chains and submerges the Egyptian chariots? ... the sky above us was silent and empty: he (God) allowed the Polish ghettos to be exterminated...'

For many devout Jews, the expectation of God's help in the hour of danger was firmly based on the themes of their own saving history: the deliverance from slavery in Egypt, the return of the exiles from Babylon, as well as the miraculous deliverance of King Hezekiah and the Holy City from the powerful armies of Assyria. And the celebration of the liturgy (especially Passover) reiterated this emphasis, while of course, also intimating that great catastrophes had struck down their ancestors because of sin and infidelity to God. But none of these thoughts prepared us or them for what overwhelmed them in Auschwitz, when millions of ordinary decent people were slaughtered. Were they to imagine suddenly that they all must have been great sinners because of what was happening to them? The tendency to look for hidden sins after the disaster has struck is, unfortunately, quite prevalent in ancient ways of thinking. It surfaced also after the Irish potato famine (1847), and was refuted in the poem, *Na Prátaí Dubha*, (The Black Potatoes), by Máire Ní Dhroma of Ring, a devout lady of independent spirit who rejected the view of some people who interpreted the famine as a divine punishment. Máire replied:

Ní hé Dia a cheap riamh an obair seo
Daoine bochta a chur le fuacht is le fán.
(It was not God who thought up this deed
To put poor people wandering out into the cold.)

If we compare the Jewish Passover liturgy with Jesus' celebration of the Last Supper (and the Christian liturgy of the eucharist), we notice a radical difference in perspective. Jesus celebrated his Last Supper around the time of the Jewish Passover. But while the Jewish Passover celebrates the deliverance of the people from slavery and death, Jesus, in his Passover, did not seek deliverance from death, in fact he pledged to offer his life in a cruel death. The Paschal mystery, for Christians, is the grain of wheat that must first fall into the ground and die before it can bear fruit. Jesus, in his preaching, never held out any hope that God would intervene directly to put down the wicked. While he performed miracles of healing for sick people, he is never reported to have worked a miracle which stopped an evil man from injuring or killing another. When faced with human wickedness (as in the person of Zacchaeus) Jesus called men to repentance, but did not exterminate them. And Jesus himself never refers to the great salvation events of Exodus, return from Exile, deliverance of Jerusalem as paradigms of political hope. The deliverance Jesus brings is not from physical death and oppression but from spiritual corruption.

The passion and death of Jesus is the supreme example, for Christians, of the persecution of the innocent by the wicked, in which there was no deliverance from death. It was also the most difficult single reality to which Jesus' followers had to adjust their thinking about God's kingdom. Their hopes were, until the last minute, for a political kingdom – a very understandable attitude in the circumstances.

In St John's account of the passion of Jesus there are two sayings unparalleled in the synoptics, both of them relevant to our topic.

Jesus, speaking in Jerusalem on what we now call Palm Sunday, is clearly aware that his hour has come, the 'hour' of his death and glorification, in which he, like the grain of wheat that falls to the earth and dies, must face the sufferings of humiliation and death, and he does not conceal his distress at what looms before him:

Now is my soul troubled. And what shall I say? 'Father, save me from this hour'? No, for this purpose I have come to this hour. Father glorify thy name. (Jn 12:27).

The 'temptation' to pray for deliverance from a cruel death is resisted. Jesus is resolved to face death. There is no prayer for a legion of angels to intervene to save the Son of God from the plots of his enemies. Why not?

Staying with the fourth gospel – the business of harmonising John with the synoptics who give us a conditional prayer for deliverance – 'if it be possible' – is not my concern now, as it would distract us from the theological intensity of the fourth evangelist's concentration on the mystery of the kingship of Jesus, which is uniquely revealed in his death – staying then with the fourth gospel, as I say, we find another logion of Jesus (again without parallel in Syn): speaking to Pilate during his trial Jesus says: 'My kingship is not of this world; *if my kingship were of this world, my servants would fight*, that I might not be handed over to the Jews; but my kingship is not from the world.' (Jn 18:36) (italics mine).

I have written in italics the words that speak of the non-violence of Jesus in the face of the hostility of his killers. And Jesus gives the reason for his non-violence: the nature of his kingship is different from that of worldly principalities and powers. And this also means that even though God does not intervene to save his Son from a cruel death, in no way does it imply that God has abandoned his Son. (John does not quote 'My God, why hast thou forsaken me? ' – perhaps to avoid misunderstanding). But Jesus does not make light of the terrible evil that surrounds his death. He admits that the forces of evil have now taken over and threaten him, but all this is within God's design. Jesus tells Pilate: 'You would have no power over me, unless it had been given to you from above. He who delivered me to you' (perhaps the high priest is referred to here) 'has the greater sin.' (19:11). Pilate, a loyal official of the Empire is 'doing his best' in an impossible situation, but the greater malice is on the part of those who orchestrated the charges against Jesus. 'After this' (or possibly 'because of this') Pilate sought to release Jesus (19:12). It may well be that Pilate is the one human being in all history who had some intimation at that time of the nature of Jesus' kingship. After hearing Jesus speak, and having assessed him with the shrewd eyes of an imperial administrator, Pilate sought to release him. And when this failed, he insisted, against the urging of the highest priestly authority, in giving Jesus his kingly title. Jesus, even in death, is king, because his kingship is not of this world. St John, with faith in Christ, can see that it is precisely when Jesus is lifted up on the cross that he draws all people to himself (12:32). In Christian art the crucified is often portrayed wearing a royal crown.

The kingdom of God and of his Christ is not of this world, but it is very much *in* this world, and nowhere more powerfully than in the martyrdom of his holy people. The consoling presence of God in the passion and death of his believers is an aspect of God's kingship. But for those believers whose principal model of divine kingship is that of the ancient Exodus deliverance, there must inevitably have been the severest crisis of faith when no angel of mercy intervened in the final moments of their agony. If the annual celebration of the Passover liturgy, with its emphasis on the triumph over political enemies and escape from death, if this, I say, formed the chief component in what the people expected from God, then the foundations of their faith must have been shaken. Such liberation theology must have died with its adherents in the saddest possible way.

But the Hebrew Bible is by no means limited to such a restricted approach to the mystery of God's ways. Indeed the Hebrew Bible itself probes this very topic of the sufferings of the innocent at greater length than any of the New Testament writings. I refer, in particular, to the Book of Job. To have included the Book of Job, which challenges many of the assumptions of Torah liberation theology, into one and the same canon of the Hebrew Scriptures, flows from a deep respect for the truth, the whole truth of human experience in its glory and also in its humiliation.

Theodicy in the Book of Job

From the point of view of theodicy, there are three distinct positions adopted by Job himself in the poetic sections of the book. The first is total irreverence towards God, and the categorical denial that any divine justice is at work in the real world of human suffering. This is the theme of Job's unrestrained 'bitter complaint' (Hebrew *Śiaḥ Mar*) against God, and is found in the earlier chapters (6-12): God's secret purpose in creating man was to make him miserable; whole societies are plunged into wickedness because of the corruption of their leaders. God is responsible for the evil in human society – it is God who, according to Job, 'takes away their wisdom from the rulers of the nations, and leaves them wandering in a pathless wilderness' (12:24).

If this were Job's final position, there would be no point in looking to God for justice, but Job moves on in the following chapters (13-31) to seek out God in order to argue his case with him. In one of the most lyrical of Job's poems, he is hoping against hope that God's fury will pass and that at last the Lord will recognise Job as worthy of a fair trial:

> If only thou wouldst hide me in Sheol and conceal me till thy
> anger turns aside, if thou wouldst fix a limit for my time
> there, and then remember me!
> Then I would not lose hope, however long my service, wait-
> ing for my relief to come.
> Thou wouldst summon me, and I would answer thee; thou
> wouldst long to see the creature thou has made (14:13-15).
> (Kissane)

This ray of hope that one day the Lord will look favourably
again on Job is found in three other little poems, each consisting of
only a few verses:

> For look, my witness is in heaven; there is one on high ready
> to answer for me. My appeal will come before God, while my
> eyes turn again and again to him (16:19, 20).

A verse better known from Handel's aria, *I know that my Redeemer
liveth*, in the oratorio *Messiah*, concerns the *go'el* (Hebrew for the vindicator or defender) who will uphold Job's good name in court –
something more precious to Job than health or wealth:

> But I know in my heart that my defender lives and that he
> will rise at last (to speak for me) 19:25.

Finally, in chapter 31, Job still speaks of God who will 'acknowledge his integrity' (31:6), and prays:

> O, that I had one to hear my case. Here is my final word, Let
> the Almighty answer me' (31:35).

In the four poems just quoted, Job is looking for a fair trial for his
case, convinced that he will be vindicated. So, after the unrestrained
'bitter complaint' of chapters 6-12 in which Job sees no hope of justice from God, he has now (chapters 13-31) formulated a hope – still
faint – for justice, and expresses himself in the *Rib* (Hb lawsuit) pattern (*cf* 'Reverence and Irreverence in Job', *ITQ* vol. 51(1985), p 90).
This is forensic language different from the unrestrained irreverence of the earlier chapters, but still falling short of the respect due
to God which is found in prayer.

And it is this attitude of prayer, of the humility of the creature
before the Creator, that Job finally expresses in the last two stanzas
of the poem:

> 42:2 'I know that you can do all things and that no purpose of
> yours can be thwarted …'
> 42:3 'Who is this that hides counsel without knowledge?'
> Therefore I have uttered what I did not understand, things
> too wonderful for me, which I did not know.
> 42:4 Hear and I will speak;

'I will question you, and you declare to me.'

42:5 I have heard of you by the hearing of the ear, but now my eye sees you;

42:6 Therefore I melt away and am comforted in dust and ashes.'

These concluding lines of the poem are the closest Job ever comes to prayer in which he acknowledges the power of the Almighty (v.2), his own awe at the wonder of God (v.3), and at the same time his closeness to God whom he now sees (v. 5), and his being comforted in his sorrows ('dust and ashes') by God's having addressed him (v. 6).[8]

These five verses must not be taken in isolation from the divine speech (chapters 38-41) to which Job has listened attentively and from which he quotes twice (vv. 3, 4) in his reply. Job's reply is his Amen to the Lord's words.

We find then in Job's words three distinct genres – the unrestrained bitterness at the beginning, then the circumspect forensic language, and finally his prayer of reconciliation with God.

Job's final words are full of deep religious feeling, but they do not constitute 'the happy ending' of the prose Epilogue which follows. In the poem Job is still in his painful condition, but he has the consolation of God's closeness to him in his 'dust and ashes' and he has been favoured by God's self-revelation in the wonders and the dark mysteries of nature, expressed in the divine speech.

Job's prayer, at the end of the poem, is not a prayer for deliverance from pain, it is a prayer of adoration, of humility, of consoling closeness to God in the midst of the sorrows of life.

These final verses of the poem may seem too brief to constitute an important element in the very long poem of Job. But we must bear in mind that they are Job's response to the long speech of God from the whirlwind. And when God speaks, that's the end of the disputation; just as when, earlier, Job had spoken, no one else dared to speak – such was the respect accorded to the great man in ancient society:

When I had spoken, no one spoke again;

my words fell gently on them;

they waited for them, as for rain,

and drank them in like showers in spring (29:22, 23).

And again, the tone of the voice from the whirlwind – it is not the soft voice of consolation heralding an end to sorrow (as in Is 66:12-14), but the austere voice of majesty (to use Elihu's term, *qol ga ͻon*, 37:4), announcing the wonders of the Lord's works in creation. The only fitting response of the creature to this genre of divine address, is the prayer of humility, of adoration, Job's Amen to the Lord.

'To rescue the prey from the teeth of the unrighteous'
> I broke the fangs of the unrighteous, and made him drop his prey from his teeth (29:17).

This is a vivid picture of the just man rescuing the bloodied victim from the jaws of the predator – the term 'prey' in Hebrew comes from the verb 'to tear to pieces'. A last minute intervention on behalf of the victim, for which even an unbeliever might be tempted to pray, and which the three devout Hebrew youths hoped for as they were being consigned, as a holocaust, to the fiery furnace for their refusal to apostasise:

> Our God is able to deliver us from the fiery furnace; and he will deliver us out of your hand, O king. But if not, we will not serve your gods (Dan 3:17).

'But if not' – three short words express the utter helplessness of so many victims of holocausts, ancient and modern, as they faced the final moments of their martyrdom. And this is what disturbs Job, who had snatched the victim from the teeth of the wicked. Why does God not intervene?

Job, in his good times, put down the wicked, and as he says so colourfully, he 'put on righteousness as a garment; and justice, like a cloak or a turban wrapped me round' (29:14). The Lord, borrowing the metaphor of dressing oneself up ('deck yourself out') from Job, now accuses Job of simply being unable to do what he had claimed:

> 40:8 'Dare you deny that I am just or put me in the wrong, that you may be right?
> 40:9 Have you an arm like God's arm, can you thunder with a voice like his?
> 40:10 Deck yourself out, if you can, with pride and dignity, array yourself in pomp and splendour;
> 40:11 unleash the fury of your wrath, look upon the proud man and humble him;
> 40:12 look upon every proud man and bring him low, throw down the wicked where they stand;
> 40:13 hide them in the dust together, and shroud them in an unknown grave.
> 40:14 Then I in my turn will acknowledge that your right hand can save you'. (NEB)

Job had claimed two things: that he himself saved the innocent from the wicked (29:17), and that God had failed to do just this. The inference from such a comparison is that Job is more just than God, and this is precisely the opening challenge made by the Lord in his address to Job out of the whirlwind:

'do you put me in the wrong that you may be right' (40:8).

This verse, as generally translated, poses a serious difficulty in that it implies that Job's purpose in denigrating God's moral perfor- mance in the world was to establish his own high moral standard. But if there is one thing Job is really sure about it is his own right- eousness; even at the end of the debate the three friends testified to this – they ceased arguing with him 'because they saw he was right- eous in his own eyes' (32:1). Job's clear conscience is a primary datum of the poem (and of the Prologue), and is not an inference from any more ultimate premise, not even from God's failure to correct the wicked.

Whatever about this, the general message of the whole passage is clear: Job has claimed too much for himself: there is so much evil in human society that no man can suppress it. The Lord's challenge to Job is: 'Look upon every proud man and bring him low' (40:12).

Job would need divine strength ('God's arm') to bring every wickedness under control. One might say, in Job's defence, that his earlier claims were intended to refer only to his small sphere of influence, the limited territory over which he held sway. But in all the long litany of Job's mighty deeds of virtue he never mentions limitations, personal or territorial. And so, on a technicality, as it were, the Lord wins this argument.

But even if the Lord wins this argument at surface level, so to speak, a deeper and darker side of the debate has now opened up: the Lord claims to do many wonders in heaven and on earth and in the waters, but never does he claim to have 'rescued the prey from the teeth of the wicked'. In the pericope under consideration, 40:8- 14, the context was almost crying out for such an assurance, but it doesn't come. And the awkwardness of the final verse (14) is almost an embarrassing avoidance of the issue that Job had been raising all along. One might have expected the Lord to have said to Job: 'If you put down all the wickedness of the earth, I will acknowledge that you are as just as I am.' But no, something far less consequential emerges: the Lord will acknowledge that Job's power can save him- self (40: 14).

The distinguished scholar A. S. Peake is one of the few commen- tators who tries to come to grips with this problem in verse 14, and says: 'The turn of phrase is unexpected. We should rather anticipate that God would then confess that Job was worthy to take His place. This, however, is not at all what God says …'.[9]

In fact, the Lord is admitting the imperfect moral condition of the world, and implicitly agreeing with Job's main thesis that the Lord does not intervene to put a stop to human wickedness. As R. Gordis says: 'The implication seems to be that there are some corners of the world where God's sway is less than total'; but Gordis is on less sure ground when he goes on to speak about the overall implications of the divine speech: 'The harmony and beauty of the natural order suggests that there is a similar order and meaning in the moral universe.'[10]

It is fascinating to see how a great thinker like Kant, who in his essay on theodicies, *Über das Misslingen aller philosophischen Versuche in der Theodicee* (1791)[11] devotes considerable reflection to Job's case, can remark, correctly I believe, that the divine speech is a description not only of the beauty of the creation, but also of the harmful and terrible things that are in the physical order. Kant goes on to state however that even if the whole physical order has a plan, the connection between that order and the moral order remains unclear. Nevertheless God had honoured Job by speaking to him on the inscrutability (*Unerforschlichkeit*) of the creation, with its wonders and its dangers.

Job had never denied the wonder of God's cosmic power; his one complaint was that God does not use this power against the wickedness of man. The Lord spoke at great length in 38-41 of heavenly and earthly realities, but in the one short passage where he mentions human wickedness (40:8-14) he does not claim to remedy it. One can hardly avoid the conclusion that the poet who wrote the divine speech is tacitly conceding Job's case on this matter. He does it, of course, with all due discretion, as befits such a delicate subject.

Job had claimed to speak from experience when he said:

> Why do the wicked enjoy long life
> hale in old age, and great and powerful?
> The rod of God's justice does not reach them.
> They live their lives in prosperity,
> And they go down to Sheol in peace' (21:7, 9, 13).

What is remarkable here is that Job's complaint is not about his own personal sufferings. His horizons have stretched far away from his solitary agony to the pitiful condition of suffering humanity oppressed by tyrants in various parts of the world. Again, Job is speaking from experience, not his own this time, but the experience of others who had travelled far and related their experiences of the great empires of world, and had even witnessed the pomp and splendour of a tyrant's funeral:

> No one denounces his conduct to his face
> no one requites him for what he has done.
> When he is carried to his grave
> all the world escorts him, before and behind.
> The dust of earth is sweet to him
> and thousands keep watch at his tomb' (21:31-33).

Job's speech followed that of Zophar who had introduced the topic of the hybris of the man who stood 'high as the heavens', whose 'head touched the clouds' (20:6), but now lies in dust (20:11).

If Zophar could have known of the posthumous dishonouring of the tyrant – one thinks today of the removal of the coffin of Stalin from the Lenin Mausoleum to which it had been consigned with highest honours – he could have used it to weaken Job's argument somewhat. But *glasnost* seems to have been as rare and as daring in antiquity as in our own time, and Job's claim stands.

This claim is never denied by the Lord in the whole course of the divine speech, and so may be considered to have been left unchallenged. But even if the Lord is tacitly conceding Job's case in this matter, he is not agreeing with everything Job has said. The Lord explicitly corrects Job for overstating his case in the matter of his own virtuous behaviour, as if Job could put down 'every proud man' (40:12).

And the friends have also corrected Job's totally irreverent manner of speaking about God. Job could have expressed his thoughts about God's inactivity in the moral order without saying that 'God mocks at the trial of the innocent' (9:23). The poet Qohelet, some centuries after Job, could take an equally pessimistic view of God's performance without the slightest hint of irreverence:

> Again I saw all the oppressions that are practised under the sun
> And behold the tears of the oppressed,
> and they had no one to comfort them.
> On the side of the oppressors there was power,
> and there was no one to comfort them (4:1).

But even if there's no irreverence in Qohelet, neither is there any passionate quest for justice, and no appeal to God to do anything about the evil of the world. In fact, when we come to Qohelet we find something unique in the Old Testament: a reflection on human iniquity without any reference to its cause or its remedy, with no call on God to deliver the innocent or to punish the oppressor. Even

Psalm 88 – 'the saddest of all the psalms' – addresses its sorrow to God. But Qohelet reports the triumph of evil in a cool detached way, and calmly moves on to other topics, addressing the reader but not God. For Qohelet there is no temptation to pray in the face of evil.

In fact, Qohelet's chief preoccupation is not the all-pervasive evil in God's creation but the sheer boredom of life even for the man who has everything under the sun: All is vanity, emptiness.

Job, however, never forgets God. Even in his despair it is to God his cry goes out. And in the end the Lord honours Job by a word, which like the mighty whirlwind from which it came, used the voice of nature in all its majesty and mystery. It is to this word that Job responds in prayer (42:1-6), even though many questions are left unanswered, and many wounds still await their healing.

Notes:

1. Levi, Primo, *The Drowned and the Saved*, English trans. London 1988, 11.
2. Apud *Maximilian of Auschwitz*, by D. Forristal, Dublin 1982, 179.
3. Op cit, 164
4. Solzhenitsyn, A., *Day in the Life of Ivan Denisovich*, Penguin, 137-140.
5. Penguin Classics, 175.
6. *The Periodic Table*, London 1986, 52
7. The repentance of Zacchaeus brought happiness not only to himself but also to the poor people to whom he distributed half his wealth, and to the over-taxed who were repaid four-fold (Lk 19:1-10). The suppression of evil can come through miracles of grace, even if it does not come through physical miracles.
8. See Psalm 73:24-26 for the combination of bitterness, ignorance of God's ways, and final closeness to God, much the same as in Job's prayer.
9. Peake, A. S., *Job*, The Century Bible, London 1904, 334.
10. Gordis, Robert, *The Book of God and Man*, Chicago, 1978, 301, 302.
11. *Kants Werke*, Walter de Gruyter, Berlin 1968. Vol. 8, 266: 'Denn Gott wurdigt Hiob, im die Weisheit Seiner Schopfung vornehmlich von Seiten ihrer Unerforschlichkeit von Augen zu stellen'.

CHAPTER 6

Reverence and Irreverence in Job

De Profundis

Of the many images of sorrow to emerge from the modern holocaust few can be as profoundly shocking as that told by Elie Wiesel in his book, *Night*[1] about the execution of a young boy prisoner in the concentration camp. The child ('with the face of a sad angel') was silent on the gallows while all the other prisoners were obliged to look on. Wiesel, who was among the onlookers, heard behind him a voice of a man asking 'Where is God now?', and says he heard a voice within himself answer 'Where is He? Here He is – He is hanging here on the gallows.'

The death of God. For some who had to experience these awful iniquities God – the God who did not intervene and stop the slaughter of the innocents – ceased to exist. For others however this cruel scene evoked another image, also of a young man, dying on the cross at Calvary, and again the same question arose: 'Where is God now?' And the answer this time was: 'He is hanging on the cross' – not in the sense that he had ceased altogether to exist, but that God had entered into the deepest sorrows of man, had shared death with man, in order to open a door to life – a life in the presence and love of God. But would it be proper for a Christian prisoner witnessing the death-scene of the innocent youth to offer, unsolicited, his thoughts to someone who does not share his faith? It would seem that in moments of great affliction the most fitting communication is not the dialogue of speech but the dialogue of silence. François Mauriac, in his preface to Wiesel's book, tells us that when he heard that sad story he was silent. 'I could only embrace him, weeping.' (p 11).

Silence. Not the silence of indifference or of superiority, but the silence of closeness, of compassion, of sharing the sorrow with the one who is crushed (Job 13:5). The silent and tearful embrace offers the only consolation that can reach the heart of the sufferer. Job's three friends consoled him with their tears and their silent presence: 'None of them said a word, for they saw that his sufferings

were very great' (2:13). It was only when they broke their silence
that they failed as comforters.

The comforter's great gift is his silent listening to the lamentation of the sufferer. How important to let the grief express itself,
even if sometimes the tone and the language may be offensive to
pious ears. How wise the synagogue was to select the five poems of
lamentation to be chanted on the annual commemoration of the
destruction of Jerusalem. And how appreciative of this the church
was when, for centuries, she voiced the same lamentations, in the
office of Holy Week, in the most heart-rending cadences of
Gregorian chant – now, regrettably no longer heard in the new
liturgy of Holy Week.

How important it is for the sake of human wholeness to allow
the outpouring of grief. How important a catharsis – physical and
spiritual – for the sufferer. But also for the one who only listens in
respectful silence to the sufferer. And when James Joyce had turned
away from his religious roots and, living in exile, rarely darkened
the door of a church, he would still find his way to the Holy Week
ceremonies and listen to the poems of sorrow from ancient Israel,
and watch as the candles were gradually extinguished, and darkness finally enveloped the congregation; religious poetry, plaintive
music, and the snuffling out of the candle-flames – this was the one
gentle voice from his religious past that could still speak to his
heart. And the only book of the Bible which could still mean anything to Wiesel in his night of the soul was that other great masterpiece of lamentation – the Book of Job. The genre of lamentation
may ultimately be the most important religious genre for a world of
little faith.

Three kinds of complaint

The voices of sorrow are many and varied in the poetry of the Old
Testament. In David's lament for the death of Saul and Jonathan (2
Sam 1:19-27) we have the outpouring of sorrow in a totally secular
dirge – no prayer to God, no complaint against God, and, of course,
no thought of happiness beyond death. The prophet Amos in the
eighth century BC, composes a *qinah*, when he anticipates the
destruction of the Northern Kingdom, and shows how deeply he
felt for the coming sorrows of people whom he thinks of as a
defenceless young woman, 'the virgin Israel', fallen, never to rise.

In the Book of Lamentations it is the turn of the southern kingdom to sing its own dirge on the occasion of the Babylonian captivity. In these lamentations we find the outpouring of sorrow – the

lament proper – accompanied by confession of sins, an acknowledgment that it was the great sinfulness of the nation which
brought on the destruction of the state. This conjoining of lament
and confession of sins is often found in Psalms too.

But there is another and much rarer form of lamentation in
which there is no confession of sins, but in which the poet firmly
asserts his innocence before God, and even accuses the Lord of
unfairly afflicting him. This form of lamentation is really a complaint against God, and it can be found both in Jeremiah and in Job,
but especially in the latter.

Three forms of complaint are found in brief pericopes in
Jeremiah where we can identify them and separate them more easily
than in the more expansive and tumultuous outpourings of Job,
who may indeed have been influenced by the prophet.

1. The lament for oneself, Jer 20:1418. This is like a dirge, the
lament for the dead, in theme, though not in metre. Jeremiah's
whole existence from his birth on is under the shadow of sorrow –
he would be better dead. This lament is not addressed to God, and
does not blame God for anything. It is simply a soliloquy of sadness. It is not a complaint against God.

2. The lament which seeks an answer to the problem of evil and
its triumph over good. This lament is expressed in the forensic language of a court suit, *Rib*. The complaint against God here observes
the correctness of legal process. Jer 12:1-4.

3. The lament against God in the language of outrage and insult
in which the disrespect and irreverence toward God is explicit. Jer
15:18; 20; 7.

Thus, complaint against God is found in two quite distinct
forms. Whereas Job 3 is, as we saw, a soliloquy of sorrow, a complaint, but not a complaint against God (except in 3:23), unrelieved
sorrow for one's very existence, cursing the day of birth, Job 7,
while voicing the same deep despair at the sorrow of life, is an
address to God, but since it is not a reverential form of address, it
can hardly be called a prayer in the usual sense of that word. It is, in
fact, explicitly disrespectful to God. Take, for instance, its parody of
Psalm 8 – a poem which praised the creative bounty of God. Job 7
turns that psalm into a mockery of God (vv 17-19).

Job knows that this language, addressed to God, is outrageous,
and he excuses himself in advance (as P. Dhorme says),[2] when he
confesses that his mind and heart are so disturbed with endless sorrow that he cannot restrain his irreverent reproach to God:

> I will not hold my peace
> I will speak out in the anguish of my mind
> I will complain in the bitterness of my soul (7:11).

Long before the modern holocaust, Israel had seen terrible days of suffering and death of innocent people when bitter prayers of reproach to God must have been voiced, and the question may have been raised about the orthodoxy of some of these outpourings. Staying with the Book of Job, we may notice how this problem is addressed. Job admits that the harsh words he speaks are wild and unrestrained, but seeks to find excuse for this fact in the heavy pressure of his vexation and calamity (6:2), comparing his mental condition to that induced by poison-tipped arrows which pierce the flesh of the victim, and send their poison into his bloodstream until his mind is unhinged (6:4). How unkind of his friends to sift the frenzied words of a man who has lost hope (6:24). But even if his words against God are wild and irreverent, do they indicate a turning away from God? Is the irreverence so fundamental that Job ceases to have any respect for God? No. Job's ultimate position in chapter 6 is that he would prefer death than to turn his back on God completely.

> This (i.e. my death) would still be my consolation –
> And I would be steadfast in pain that spareth not –
> That I have not denied the words of the Holy One. (6:10, Kissane)

Even if 10c – the last line – is, as some have suggested, not original (because it gives a tristich instead of a distich – this latter being the length of all except two verses in chapter 6), there is no doubt the interpolator made a theologically judicious complement to the thought of the preceding two lines. A man under great pressure realises that he is near breaking point and fears he might lose his respect for God and, so as to avoid such irreverence, would prefer to die before he utters blasphemy. This attitude bespeaks a fundamental reverence towards God. The man who feels he may be losing 'the fear of God' (10:14) and that to avoid offending God he would prefer to die first, is a deeply religious man in spite of his verbal lapses under great pressure. And we must remind ourselves that in uttering a lamentation for himself ancient man was entitled to great freedom of utterance – a healthy outpouring of grief was encouraged, and Western European cultures which frown on this custom may not be as wise as the ancients were, whose culture favoured an unrestrained catharsis, not only at the psychological level but at the religious level as well. Job's lamentation pours out not only the anguish of his broken body but of his tormented spirit as well, and in this latter context he turns his anger on God. And Job's hard words are spoken in such a context. Corrections can come when the agony is past, but while the sorrow is great he must express it – fully.

The tristich is stylistically important in chapter 6 when it is employed only twice (vv. 4, 10) in contrast to the distichs of all the other verses. There is no need to regard the third stichos (in each case) as suspect simply because it departs from the general pattern. In both verses the thought is brought forward by the third line, in harmony with, but complementary to, the thought of the earlier verses. In 6:4 Job for the first time in the poem names God explicitly as the author of his woes. The parallelism between 4a and 4c is quite clear, but the intervening 4b, though an intrusion from the point of view of poetic parallelism, has an important function poetically – it introduces the idea of the spreading of the poison from the arrow tips to the blood stream, thus deranging Job's spirit and giving rise to his frenzied words against his hunter – God!

The tristich in 6:10 is of great theological importance. Job would welcome death before his agony leads him into revolt against God because then he would die knowing he had not turned his back on God:

> I have not denied the words of the Holy One (6:10c).

I have followed Kissane's interpretation of 6:10c as giving the grounds for Job's consolation in his last agony, but even if a different interpretation is followed, viz. that 10c gives the reason why God should grant Job's request for death, we are still left with an affirmation of Job's life-long loyalty to God, and this as something very precious to him, showing that he is still a religious man.

This is the basic reverence of Job: his other utterances must be viewed not in isolation but in harmony with this basic reverence (his 'fear of God').

The third and final tristich in Job's first reply to Eliphaz is:

> Therefore I will not restrain my mouth
> I will speak in the anguish of my heart
> I will complain in the bitterness of my soul (7:11).

Job has now embarked on a more daring form of lamentation: the earlier restraint is now gone and he clearly intends the reader to be alerted to the deepening of his despair, the casting off of reverential restraints and a language more frenzied than in chapter 3. He will now address God directly (which he hadn't done in chapter 3), but his address will be positively shocking and irreverent.

The verse just quoted – again standing out because it is a tristich surrounded by distichs – is the harbinger of irreverent outpourings which include the parody on Psalm 8, and, later, Job's despair of ever getting a fair hearing before the divine tribunal, even supposing he succeeds in reaching such a point of meeting with God (9:11):

> Though I were righteous, mine own mouth would condemn me (9:20).
> (God) mocks at the trial of the innocent (9:23b).

This extreme position of Job, claiming that even in the divine tribunal God would give an unjust verdict against the innocent, is surely the low point of his irreverence. It is a position from which Job will later withdraw (23:4-7) but there is no doubt that as it stands in chapter 9 it is blasphemous. However, even here it is excusable because of Job's agony which has already become unbearable. Job has lost his patience (6:11), his strength is not that of stone nor is his flesh bronze (6:12), his inner resources have run out (6:13). If his friends had been loyal to him they might have sustained him in his agony, but they failed, and their sifting of his opening words have left him only more wounded and reduced (6:26). The result has been that he has reached breaking point and has lapsed into irreverence (in chapter 7 and following).

The third irreverence: God's secret but perverse purpose in the creation of his masterpiece, man, was to spy on his creature for any fault and then pounce on him and hold him blameworthy (10:13, 14). If God had even a spark of kindness he would let his poor creature enjoy the short spell of life left to him before he departs for ever to the grave (10:20 ff.).

In 12:13-22 we have a mocking hymn to God, the author of disorder and the perverter of justice in the world: we have again the biting sarcasm and irreverent mockery of the divine Judge. In chapter 12 we have reached the lowest point of disdain for God. When the supreme judge of the cosmos uses his power to make counsellors behave like idiots, and drives judges mad (12:17), and takes away the discretion of elders (12:20), and leads people astray (12:23); when God deprives the rulers of the world of their wisdom (12:24), then there is no hope of justice either in heaven or on earth.

But from chapter 13 on, Job finds an emerging hope that God will eventually grant him justice (a fair hearing). From the total negativity of chapter 12 we move bit by bit to a positive approach to God. In chapter 13 there is a change of mood. A new calm supersedes the great storm of chapter 12. As R. E. Murphy says, 'The transitional character of 13:1-5 is marked by its academic character:

sages dispute with one another, and Job announces his intention of pleading his case before God'.[3]

In chapter 13 reason and calm has replaced the fury of the hurricane of abuse. The appeal for justice is taken up with fresh composure of spirit and gradually builds up until Job's final appeal for a 'hearer' (31:35-37). The problem is still real but Job is facing it with the precision of the legal process or *Rib* (lawsuit).

In spite of the change in mood from chapter 12, Job still has great sorrows to bear: the shortness of his life, the ongoing pain and humiliation from his so-called friends. These are still with him and he freely laments their burden on his soul, but he never again resorts to the kind of irreverent insult to God which culminated in chapter 12. It is not sufficient to say Job is simply contradicting himself. There is a modal contradiction, surely, between chapter 12 and chapter 13, and the tone of each chapter is different – they come out of totally different conditions of soul. Their 'setting in the psyche' is different. Job, from chapter 13 on, is coming closer to the respectful Job of the Prologue, at least in the sense that he now respects God even if he is impatient with his lot in life – his impatience in chapter 13 is clearly directed at his former friends – who now are identified with 'enemies' – formerly God was the great enemy (6-12).

Whereas the literary genre of the mocking *śiaḥ* dominated Job's utterances in 6-12, the *Rib* genre dominates the next section 13-21. The lament genre is present also in 13-31 but the wild irreverence to God no longer figures in it.

But although chapter 13 is the turning point, it sets out, tentatively at first, on a new road towards God in search of justice. The first intimation that Job might find justice in God is in the threat to the friends whom Job accuses of deliberate deceit in their charges against him, a fault which God himself will punish:

Will you speak falsely for God
And speak deceitfully for him?
Will you show partiality toward him,
Will you plead the case for God? ... (13:7, 8)
He will surely rebuke you,
If in secret you show partiality (13:10).

Job is now looking to God as the guardian of justice – a far cry from the Hymn to the God of Chaos (12:13-25).

More explicitly, in regard to his own dispute with God which is still unresolved, Job has positive hopes of a just verdict:

This will be my salvation
That a godless man shall not come before him (13:16).

Behold I have prepared my case; I know I shall be vindicated
(13:18).

From chapter 13 on, the theme of a just trial predominates, and
the hopes for a heavenly witness (16:19) and a defender (*goʾel*,
19:35), and a 'hearer' (31:35) are aspects of this theme. The presup-
position is that God, when confronted with the full evidence of
Job's innocence, will grant a just verdict of acquittal, and this pre-
supposition is eventually explicitly stated in 23:7:

There (at the divine tribunal) an upright man could reason
with him, And I should be acquitted for ever by my judge.

Chapter 13 then sees a change of mood, of theme and of vocabulary (now related to a fair trial where not merely Job but his friends
will be subjected to scrutiny – this latter motif quite new).

One very important consequence of this change of genre from
'bitter lamentation' to controlled legal argument is that Job's assertion of God's injustice will have been affirmed in two totally distinct literary genres – in the *śiaḥ mar* (chapter 12) and in the *Rib*
(chapter 13), to stay with Job's own terminology – instead of impos-
ing another on his utterances.[4] Chapters 13-31 show us the calmer
Job whose considered opinion is set out in the more nuanced language of the legal form.

Job's Lawsuit against God
a)   O, that I had one to hear (my case)
        Here is my taw (i.e. my last word),
        Let the Almighty answer me.
        And the scroll which my Adversary has written –
        Surely on my shoulder I would carry it,
        And wear it like a crown on my head;
        I would give him an account of all my life
        I would present it like a prince. (31:35-37)
        He will weigh me in a just balance,
        God will acknowledge my integrity (31:6, my translation).

Job has a complaint against God (27:2), and is now (31:35-37)
seeking a judicial hearing at which he will present his case. He is
confident that if the Lord would only listen to his complaint he (Job)
would be acquitted. He asks for a 'hearer', a *shomea*ʾ, one who
would be competent to hear his case and give judgment on it. This
forensic use of the noun *shomea*ʾ can be found in other texts of the
Old Testament, and perhaps a look at 2 Sam 15:1-6 will supply an
interesting parallel to the Joban passage (31:35-37). Absalom made
a point of seeking out any citizen who had a *rib* (controversy, law-

suit) which he was taking to the king's tribunal. Absalom would
say to him: 'See, your claims are good and right, but there is no
shomea' ('hearer') deputed by the king to hear your case' (15:3). The
'hearer' in this passage is clearly not just any listener, but one
deputed to hear and pass judgment on behalf of the king. We may
note that no mention is made of any adversary who might oppose
the man with the case. The case may have concerned taxation or
military service or treason or some other matter which could not be
resolved at the local assembly 'at the gate'. Certain matters had to
go before the king's tribunal.[5] In practice the king or, more likely,
his agent was the adversary, but the king was, in theory, ideally just
and a source of just judgment for his subjects; and a citizen who felt
he had been unfairly treated by a royal official was within his rights
in appealing to the royal tribunal.[6] The citizen then who felt he was
unfairly treated by a royal official had, ideally at any rate, recourse
to the king's tribunal where various officers were competent to hear
and judge the case in the name of the king (*cf* Jer 26:1-19 where 'the
princes' who came from the royal palace in Jerusalem to hear the
evidence of the priests and prophets against Jeremiah gave a judgment of acquittal in his case). In practice however a citizen could be
left unheard – as in 2 Sam 15.

If we return to Job we can see how closely his situation resem-
bles that of the man whom Absalom met on his way to the king's
tribunal. Job wants to put his case to the Almighty and he is convinced that if only the Almighty heard his case he would acquit
him: Job says:

Oh, that I knew where I might find him
that I might come even to his *seat*
I would lay *my case* before him
and fill my mouth with arguments.
I would learn what he would *answer* me.
Would he contend with me in the greatness of his power?
No; he would give heed to me.
There an upright man could reason with him,
And I should be acquitted for ever by *my judge*.
(23-1-7; cf. 13:18)[7]

In spite of all his sufferings Job has faith in the justice of the
Almighty – if only God could hear Job's case! But Job has not succeeded in meeting God (23:8 f).

Here we may notice a certain difficulty. While the king himself
may be the essence of justice, his many servants who carry out his
policies may be guilty of injustice in dealing with the king's sub-

jects, but since they act as the king's agents the king is ultimately responsible for their excesses. So also in the case of the Almighty and his ministers. This is made clear in the Prologue: the Lord's rebuke to Satan, 'you incited me against him to destroy him without cause' (2:3). The implication is that the Lord was less than pleased with the severity of Satan's treatment of Job ('... to destroy him') and, at the same time, accepts responsibility for that treatment ('you incited me against him'). That the Lord uses secondary agents in carrying out his designs is a widely held belief in the Old Testament, and that these agents may go beyond the fair measure is occasionally attested. Thus both Assyria and Babylonia overstepped the divine commission to punish Judah and will be chastised for this excess (Is 10:5-8; 47:6). As Elphaz says: 'even his angels he (i.e. God) charges with error' (4:18b).[8] But those who (like Job) are at the receiving end of such errors at the hands of God's agents are entitled to call out to God for redress and vindication of their rights, and to lay the blame where ultimately it belongs – at the door of the Almighty. The implication is that once the Almighty is presented with the evidence of the evil he will deliver the innocent from the oppression. What Job is crying out for is not mercy but justice.

Job's strong language against God must not be taken in isolation from his search for God's tribunal. The two things are aspects of the *rib* or legal suit. Job is blaming God for cruelty and injustice but is also searching for the same God to correct the injustice, and in this he is acknowledging God as the source of justice. The harsh language taken by itself might indicate a turning away from God, but if taken as the preface to a plea for divine justice it is ultimately an acknowledgment of God as the deliverer (*go'el.* 19:25) and the just judge who hears (31:35) and answers the cry of the oppressed. Job is using the model of the royal tribunal (as in 2 Sam 15:1-6), and the 'answer' he expects (23:5; 31:35) is not that of a hostile adversary, but of a just judge who would vindicate him.

Whether God is himself the 'hearer' or appoints some trusted servant to administer justice in his name is not possible to determine. In the latter case the official acts in the name of the king – and so the king may be said to have heard the case. This is the situation in 2 Sam 15, where the man came to the king for judgment, but was disappointed because no *shomea'* had been appointed to hear his case and give judgment.

Job's wish in 31:35-37 that someone would hear his case comes near the end of his last great soliloquy with its long list of imprecatory oaths, and, of its very nature, an oath is an act of trust in the righteousness of God. Job is turning to God for justice, as he was in 19:25 where the *go'el* is the equivalent to the *shomea'* of 31:35. In an interesting parallel from Egypt[9] we find the same use of the verb 'to hear' not followed by a direct object: an obscure official of the Sixth Dynasty named Uni rose in favour to the rank of judge, and he says: 'I heard ... in the name of the king'. There seems to be good reason, then, for identifying the 'hearer' of Job 31:35 with the judge appointed by the Almighty to hear Job's case and to issue a verdict in the name of the Almighty. In this sense it could be said that the Almighty answered Job (31:35b).

A parallel, from Egyptian legal texts,[10] concerns the trial of an innocent coppersmith who had confessed, under torture, to stealing 'a few things' from the royal tombs, but who later was found to be innocent. The judges who examined him the second time required him to take an imprecatory oath (like Job's in chapter 31), acquitted him, reinstated him in his office, and issued their favourable judgment in a scroll. In both cases we are dealing with the trial of the innocent, who has already been unjustly dealt with by a high official (of the Pharaoh or of God) and who brings his case to a royal/divine tribunal, where a high official is deputed to hear the case in the name of the king/God. In both cases the verdict is written on a scroll. One final illustration from Egyptian legal parallels to Job is so fascinating as to merit our attention: it is taken from the inscription of Uni, already referred to. The high point in the 'from rags to riches' career of this once petty official came when he was appointed sole judge in the delicate matter of the prosecution of the queen: again we may note his appointment by the king, his 'hearing' (the case – understood, not expressed), and his issuing the verdict in written form, this last act being a special prerogative of the presiding judge:

> When *legal procedure was instituted in private* in the harem *against the queen*, Imtes (*Ymts*) *his majesty caused me* to enter, *in order to hear (the case) alone. I alone was the one who put (it) in writing*, together with a single judge.[11]

Similarities between chapter 31 and the Egyptian Book of the Dead have often been noted. In the Egyptian text[12] the deceased presents himself before the God Osiris, to be judged. Like Job, the deceased addresses Osiris directly with protestations of innocence. After this he addresses the forty-two lesser gods present. Osiris uses a scales in which the character of the deceased is weighed (*cf* Job 31:6). Job 31:36 also refers to a written scroll – the only example in the Old Testament of the use of such a written (as distinct from oral) testimony, another Egyptian practice. Both Job and the Egyptian man are asking for justice not mercy, and both look on the deity as just.

The Egyptian says to Osiris:

Lord of Justice is thy name.

Job says:

There an upright man could reason with him (i.e. God), and I should be acquitted for ever by my judge (23:7).

But there are also differences between the Egyptian text and Job, both as to form and content. The form of the Egyptian address to Osiris is negative confession, e.g. 'I have not committed evil against men' while that of Job is that of imprecatory oath: 'If I have raised my hand against the fatherless ... then let my shoulder blade fall from my shoulder' (31:21, 22). But, more importantly, while the Egyptian text involves many *dramatis personae*, with the deceased addressing many divine personages, some of whom speak to him directly (p. 36), Job is all alone, with no awareness of any judge listening to his pleadings, and this is the very reason for his wishing for a 'hearer'. The Joban poet has reduced the naïve mythical trappings of the older Egyptian scenery and left us with a bare stage in the manner of Samuel Beckett in which a solitary man speaks his monologue.

b) 'The heavenly witness' (16:19)

Even now behold my witness is in heaven,

and he that vouches for me is on high ...

that he would maintain the right of a man with God

like that of a man with his neighbour (16:19, 21 RSV).

Chapter 16 is important for the overall interpretation of Job's approach to his problems. He feels quite sure that he has only a few more years to live, but while his only wish in chapter 3 was that death might come soon and put him out of agony, he now prays, not for forgiveness, nor for a return to health, but for the vindication of his innocence, the restoration of his good name in the eyes of his friends, who have maligned him. For Job the highest human value is that of the innocent conscience, but he is not a solipsist, but a man for whom social reality and recognition is essential to happiness. He is also a religious man who wishes to be accepted for what he is by God, and to come close to God – this final wish is realised only at the very end of the poem (42:5, 6), in which Job, though still seriously ill, finds consolation in God, a consolation to which his relatives and former acquaintances added their voices when they came to him and 'sympathised with him and comforted him for all the evil the Lord had brought upon him' (42:11). This verse just quoted brings to an end the consolation theme so important in the Book of Job. This same verse (42:11) may thus be the original ending of the Epilogue, the remaining verses which give the 'happy ending', (viz. 42:10-17, excluding v. 11) being a secondary addition giving a more material dimension to the high spirituality of the original ending.'[13]

In 16:19-22, then, Job combines a fervent hope that a heavenly witness will vindicate his good name before the throne of the Almighty. The function of the heavenly witness is sometimes compared to that of witness for the defence, but is more correctly seen as a witness to the truth. Since Job stresses his own truthfulness so much, and since he is convinced of his innocence, then in practice the heavenly witness will defend Job. The imagery of a heavenly trial at which a truthful witness would plead for an innocent man before God is quite exceptional in the Old Testament. Job seems to be drawing on Egyptian models such as are found in the address of the deceased at the judgement before Osiris,when the deceased calls on the forty-two lesser gods to testify to his innocence:

> Behold me – I have come to you without sin, without guilt, without evil, without a witness (against me). I have given bread to the hungry, water to the thirsty, clothing to the naked, and a ferry-boat to him who was marooned. (So) rescue me, you; protect me, you.[14]

There is considerable similarity between the two worlds of thought here – between the Joban and the Egyptian texts. The emphasis on the innocence of the man on trial, the emphasis on the primacy of the truthfulness both in the man and in the heavenly witnesses, the distinction between the witnesses and the supreme judge (Osiris, God). Some scholars identify the heavenly witness in Job 16:19 with God, but verse 21 is clearly hostile to such an interpretation. Analogies from Babylonian personal gods who would defend their client before the high gods are also adduced, but Babylonian personal religion puts the emphasis on ritual rather than moral performance, whereas the Egyptian funerary texts place the main emphasis on moral obligations. The whole atmosphere then, combining innocence, truthfulness, and finally the implication of the absolute fairness of the supreme judge, is common to the Joban scenario as well as to the Egyptian view of judgment. And we are not depending solely on written texts with regard to the Egyptian thought. In Egyptian funerary art the beautifully coloured interiors of royal tombs and of mastabas reveal a judgment scene marked by order, serenity, objectivity, with the accurate balancing of the scales in which the heart of the deceased will be weighed (*cf* Job 31:6). In this respect the ancient Egyptians had perhaps an ethically superior notion of the great judgment than that displayed by the fearful faces in Michelangelo's great Sistine fresco. And Job stands confident that his integrity will be recognised by the Almighty, and this is his greatest act of respect and reverence for God. In this he has 'spoken well of God' (42:7, 8).

But there is one important difference between the Joban heavenly court and its Egyptian counterpart. The man on trial in the Egyptian scene is already dead; Job, on the contrary, is still living on this earth. The Joban poet did not have to travel outside his own religious culture for the imagery he needed to meet this requirement. Psalm 7 could have supplied him with the following elements:

1. The speaker is innocent, and affirms this with an imprecatory oath (7:3-5).

2. He is falsely accused by enemies (7:3).

3. He appeals to a divine tribunal (7:6) not for an eschatological judgment after death; but for a judgment in the present world of good and evil.

4. He explicitly recognises the Lord as a righteous judge, and on this ground he looks for a vindication of his innocence (7:8, 11).

All these are part of the scenario for Job 16:19, and they indicate Job's respect and reverence for God as righteous. Once again the model of the royal tribunal to which the innocent man may, with impunity, make his complaint, seems best suited to safeguard the basic reverence for the Almighty as the ultimate guardian of righteousness.

Conclusion
Among the many laments of the Old Testament those of Job hold a special place for the intensity and bitterness of their dark accusal of God. This feature of irreverence has been the special object of this study, and in the interests of clarity we may set out again the three different kinds of complaint in Job.

1. Job's opening complaint is a soliloquy of sorrow, cursing the day of his birth (chapter 3, like Jer 20:14-18). This is not, explicitly at any rate, a complaint against God. It is a complaint about the sadness of life and is a song of despair, seeing no hope of return to health, and wishing for death. It is like a dirge except that while in a dirge the poet laments some one else's death, here he weeps for

himself as one very close to death. He does not pray to God for deliverance, in fact quite the opposite – he wishes that death would end his agony. And this is exactly how Eliphaz understands it when very skilfully he tries to win his despairing friend to pray to God for restoration to health (chapters 4, 5). From the point of view of religious orthodoxy, no charge of irreverence to God can be made against Job on the evidence of his opening soliloquy, nor does his friend Eliphaz suggest as much. It is only when we move on to the other two kinds of complaint that this charge may be made.

But staying for the moment with the opening complaint of Job we may note that not merely does it contain the fulsome expression of great sorrow, but it also gives free vent to his anger, expressed in his cursing the day of his birth, calling up the occult forces of evil to blot out from the calendar the day he was born and the night he was conceived (3:3). David's dirge also included not merely his sorrow but also his anger and curse on the place of the slaying of his two friends, and Jeremiah's lament for his own sad life likewise curses the man who brought the news of his birth (20:15), and lapses into unspeakable impiety by picturing his own mother in the perpetual distension of her pregnancy, 'my mother, my tomb' (Jer 20:17). Even in the most poignant lyrics of personal lament coming from the period of the ancient holocaust (sixth century BC) the most appalling vindictiveness can erupt in crying out for the smashing of the infants of the persecutors on the pavements (Ps 137:8, 9). Nevertheless this pathetic cry of sorrow and anger may not be silenced by those who themselves have never been singed by the flames of the furnace. The call on the survivors of holocausts, ancient and modern, to forgive and forget may be insensitive to the depth of the wounds of the surviving remnant, wounds which, as we now know, even after forty years, may not have healed. Insensitive too to the hidden flames which may still burn in the inmost recesses of their brains. Insensitive, finally, to the important truth that the majority of those who might have forgiven have had their voices stilled for ever in the furnace, and that no one else can legitimately speak for them. Perhaps in God's own good time, in God's own time of healing ... but we must stay with Job for the moment.

The lament genre, of its very nature, is open and unrestrained in its outpouring of both grief and anger. For bystanders to try to restrain the sufferer from expressing his grief and his anger because of the impropriety of the language of lament is to add further sorrow to the afflicted person, and this is precisely what Job finds disloyal in his three friends, if we may follow M. Pope's translation of

6:14:

> A sick man should have loyalty from his friend,
> Though he forsake the fear of the Almighty.

Nevertheless the free expression of anger against 'enemies' can take a turn for the worse when a curse (or a serious accusal) is uttered not just against a battle-field, nor against the man who announced the birth, but against God himself. And while Job never cursed God, he did utter explicit complaints against God in two distinct literary forms. It is to those that we must now once again turn our attention.

2. The bitter outbursts of Job against God which we find in 12:14-25 and elsewhere constitute a genre of unrestrained taunt of blasphemous intent, which can only be excused by reason of the overwhelming anguish of a man who has reached breaking point, and is now speaking out of his agony. This is the approach of the ancient Rabbis to such language, and it is in conformity with Job's own understanding of his wild words (6:11; 13:13; 17:11): his reverence for God is still so strong that he would prefer death to come before he lapses into such blasphemy (6:10).

3. The second form of complaint against God is more restrained than that above. It is an accusal against God presented in the request for a lawsuit (*Rib*). This request, and its accompanying complaint, is set out in the correct language appropriate to the law courts (like Jer 12:1-4), with the reflective calm and respect of a plaintiff who looks for a favourable verdict from a just judge. But the plaintiff has, nevertheless, a difficult complaint to make, viz. that he has been treated unjustly by God.

The three basic elements in Job's *rib* against God are: Job is an innocent man: God is the ultimate source of justice; but Job is being unjustly afflicted – by God (or his agent). It is remarkable that only in the Prologue are these three elements explicitly highlighted. In the Prologue, God is the just judge who gladly acknowledges the innocence of Job; Job is indeed upright and religious; but Satan, who operates within certain limits imposed by God, is nevertheless capable of inflicting immense hurt and sorrow on the innocent. Satan is therefore the heavenly counterpart of the oppressive royal official against whose actions the innocent can appeal to the supreme judge. The function of the Prologue is far more nuanced than the contrasting of its patient Job with the angry Job of the dialogue, and M. Buttenwieser's judicious words on the 'subtle harmony' by which Prologue and dialogue are bound together have merit.[15] Job, of course, shows no explicit awareness of Satan, but is quite sure that agents of evil are at work against him, and against these he hopes for God's aid (17:1-9). Even though Job cries out against God he is also quite explicit that he has other enemies, distinct from God, but nevertheless subject in some way to the overall control of God. Evil in the world, therefore, is not directly an infliction of the Lord himself upon an innocent Job: a whole host of intermediatories, working with their own limited but real dynamic and initiative, can cause immeasurable sorrow to the innocent. A judgment on all this complexity of evil is countenanced in the model of the royal tribunal to which the innocent may appeal for eventual justice from the supreme judge.

Touching the matter of reverence and irreverence, the use of the model of the royal tribunal is directly relevant to the evaluation of Job's accusations against God. It is correct and proper for the innocent party to voice his grievance against the king's administration in a forthright and explicit way before the royal tribunal. Even if the innocent party has an overly high estimation of his own integrity (as Job has) and an exaggerated expectation of what society (or God) owes him, he is entitled to speak his mind, and it is up to the court to correct the plaintiff's overstatements (*cf* 40:2, 8) without, however, rejecting his right to plead. Job is entitled, therefore, to state his case before the heavenly tribunal, and to make his accusations against God's hard ways of dealing with him. He is doing so in the firm conviction that when God listens to Job's own statement of his case he will grant him a just acquittal. This conviction of Job that God is the final source of justice is ultimately the factor which stamps Job's pleas as reverent.

Notes:
1. Eng. trans., New York, 1960, 76
2. *Le Livre de Job* (Paris, 1926), in loco.
3. *The Forms of the Old Testament Literature*, vol XIII (Grand Rapids, 1981) 30
4. The Hebrew term *síaḥ* means 'musing', 'complaint'; the adjective *mar* means 'bitter', and in Job refers not to any passing irritation bu; to the deepest frustration of soul, which can arise when a man of high moral character is deprived of his rights (27:2), and for whom death would now be a happy release:

> Why is light given to him that is in misery,
> and life to the bitter of soul,
> who long for death, but it comes not ...? (3:20, 21a).

The phrase 'bitterness of soul' is important therefore as a key to the psychological ground from which Job's lamentations flow (7:11; 10:1), and Job uses a number of very rare words derived from the root *mar* which have the implications of 'poisonous' (16:13; 20:14; 25) – as if the poison of his wounds has deranged his mind, and caused him to cry out in sorrow and anger (6:4).

5. *Cf* Boecker, H. J., *Law and the Administration of Justice in the Old Testament and Ancient East* (London, 1980) 40-49. Alt, A., *Essays*, Oxford, 1966, 101

6. *Cf* 1 Kings 3:9 where Solomon prays for 'a hearing heart' – indicating the king's willingness to hear a case before giving judgement – and this ideal of the just king who administers just judgement is also enshrined in the messianic hopes of Isaiah chapters 9 and 11.

7. One may note that this passage contains no mention of an adversary. The words underlined indicate that the Almighty is the judge before whose tribunal Job presents his case and who will answer Job with a favourable verdict. The Almighty would thus be Job's *go 'el* (19:35) and *shomea '* (31:35).

8. Compare the prayer of the Egyptian deceased to Osiris to rescue him from the God's messengers (*ANET*, 36). See below.

9. Breasted, J.H., *Ancient Records of Egypt* (Chicago, 1906), vol 1, par 307.

10. Op cit, vol IV, pars 524 and 534: 'The nobles examined the coppersmith with a severe examination in the great valley, (but) he was not found to know any place there, except the two places upon which he had laid his hand. He took an oath of the King, L. P. H., that he should be mutilated (by cutting off) his nose and his ears and placed upon the rack (if he lied), saying: "I know not any place here among these tombs except this tomb which is open, together with the hut upon which I have laid your hands".

534. The great nobles granted life to the coppersmith of 'The-House-of-Usermare-Meriamon,'L.-P.-H.,-(in-the-House-of)-Amon.' They were reassigned to the High Priest of Amon-Re (king of gods), Amenhotep, on this day.

The documents thereof are: one roll; it is deposited in the office of the vizier's archives.'

11. Italics mine in this paragraph 310 from Breasted, J. H., op. cit. vol 1.

12. *ANET*, p 34

13. *Cf* Buttenwieser, M., *The Book of Job* (London 1922) 67.

14. *ANET*, 35.

15. Op cit 26-30. But even the so-called contradiction between the characterisations of Job as patient (in the Prologue) and the angry Job (in the dialogue) should not be pressed. Even a patient man who maintained his integrity throughout two terrible trials could, after a further prolongation of his agony (-seven days) and provocation from his former friends, find himself at breaking point and then utter rash words against his better judgment.

CHAPTER 7

The Happy Ending

At the very beginning of the Russian text of Tolstoy's novel *Anna Karenina* the word 'house' occurs eight times in six sentences. But, strange as it may seem, the word 'house' occurs only once in some English translations of this passage, once in the French, and only twice in the Czech, according to Milan Kunderal who adds: 'Translators are crazy about synonyms', and, may I add, are sometimes so embarrassed by repetitions in the original, that they try to improve on it. V. Nabokov, whose shrewd eyes spotted Tolstoy's eight 'houses', had no doubt, however, that the repetition was a deliberate tactic of the author who wished his reader to notice it and reflect on its implications. In other words, the repetitions are the work of the cunning hand of the artist, and not a token of his impoverished vocabulary.

This brings me to the two verses in Job which have more repetitions than any other passage in that great book. It comes towards the very end of the book, immediately after the poetry, where Job, having listened to the majestic nature poem of the Lord out of the whirlwind, admits that the Creator's ways are beyond the mind of man. The Epilogue then begins (42:7): 'And it came to pass after the Lord had spoken these words to (or 'concerning') Job, the Lord said to Eliphas the Temanite, 'My anger is hot against you and against your friends, because *you have not spoken concerning me what is right, as my servant Job has done.'* (42:8): 'So now, take seven bulls and seven rams, go to *my servant Job* and offer a whole-burnt offering for yourselves, and let *my servant Job* intercede for you; for I will accept him, so that I may not do anything rash to you; for *you have not spoken concerning me what is right, as my servant Job has done.'*

I have taken the liberty of italicising 'my servant Job' which occurs four times in the Hebrew text, but only twice in the English of the NEB. I have also italicised the whole phrase 'you have not spoken concerning me what is right' which occurs in 42:7 and again in the following verse (8b).

These repetitions have drawn down on the head of the Hebrew

author the following now often quoted reproach from the distinguished commentators Driver-Gray: 'If the whole of the Epilogue and Prologue are from the same hand, that hand has lost its cunning before it reached the Epilogue; the repetition of 8b of the clause in 7b may indeed be a mere textual accident: if not, it is very different in character from the repetitions in the Prologue; but the contrast comes out more strangely in the absence of concentration and compression which contributes so largely to the effect of the Prologue. We may note especially the irrelevant particularity which gives the names of Job's daughters, and the detail as to their inheritance …' (ICC, Edinburgh, 1921, 373).

'My servant Job' occurs four times in these two verses of the Epilogue, and twice in the Prologue (1:8; 2:3), and nowhere else in the whole Book of Job. It comes always from the lips of the Lord and is always spoken as a term of special honour for Job: 'there is no one like him on earth, a man of blameless and upright life', and it indicates Job's loyalty to his Lord in good times (1:8) and bad times (2:3). In fact, however, the test of Job's loyalty to his Lord hinges on how he will speak of the Lord; will it be by blessing God or cursing him? The whole suspense of the Prologue concerns Job's words after his first ordeal, and then after his second. The author deliberately delays Job's final utterances until the end of both trial scenes (1:21; 2:10). And after Job has spoken well of the Lord, the narrator confirms Job's loyalty by stating negatively what Job has spoken positively (1:22; 2:10c): Job did not sin with his lips (2: 10).

The importance of what Job says in adversity is further emphasised by putting on his lips the only genuinely poetic passage in the Prologue-Epilogue:

> Naked I came from my mother's womb,
> and naked shall I return thither.
> The Lord has given, the Lord has taken away,
> May the name of the Lord be blessed (1:21).

These poetic words are not addressed directly to God; but they are spoken concerning God's ways and they call on all who hear Job to join with him in pronouncing the name of the Lord as blessed. And so, when we finally reach the Epilogue, and rejoin the prose narrative begun in the Prologue, the author of both Prologue and Epilogue (who may well also be the author of the poem) deliberately uses repetition in 42:7, 8 to bring us back to where he broke off in 2:13.

The four-fold 'my servant Job' (42:7, 8) rings a bell immediately: Where did I hear that honorific title before? Why, way back in the

Prologue, and nowhere else. And in what way did the servant Job display his loyalty? Why, by speaking properly concerning the Lord and his ways with men. But when the Lord addressed Job in the poem, he had anything but praise for Job's words. In fact, the opposite:

> Who is this whose ignorant words cloud my design in darkness? (38:2) NEB.

The Job of the poem (as distinct from the Job of the prose) admits that he has spoken of things he did not understand (42:3), and thus accepts the Lord's rebuke.

There is no sensible way the Lord's commendation of Job's words in the Epilogue (42:7, 8) could refer to anything Job said in the *poem*. Only in the *prose* legend does Job speak well of God.

What of the silence of the friends, as for seven days and seven nights they shared Job's sorrow by sitting with him on the ground, 'and no one spoke a word to (or 'concerning') him' (2:13)?

Although 2:13 gives the impression that the friends didn't speak a word to Job, the previous verse indicates that 'they lifted up their voice and wept', using two verbs that almost certainly indicate articulate speech such as might be used by mourners expressing their grief. While the use of a higher pitch for the voice ('lifting up') may be indicated, the use of fairly stereotyped formulae of grief may well be present. A very close parallel may be found in the Keret legend from Ugarit where the king's daughter, concerned for her father's illness,

> uttered her voice in *weeping* (*bky*):
> 'We rejoiced in your life, our father,
> we exulted in your immortality' etc. (Keret 16 ii, 97, 98)

The son of Keret also 'utters his voice and weeps' (16 i, 13, 14) and the text immediately goes on, after 'weeps', to give direct speech of the speaker without the words 'and said' found in J. C. L. Gibson's English translation.[2] When his father answers him he tells him 'Not to weep, not to lament' (the root *dmm*, 'lament').

We have to remind ourselves that in Hebrew the verb 'to weep' (*bkh*) is different from 'shedding tears', for which Hebrew has a different verb. Weeping, in the Old Testament, is more a function of the voice than of the eyes, and would frequently express itself in articulate lament. Its effect is to indicate to the sufferer that his friends share his distress – they sympathise with him, and by sharing his sorrow they bring him a modicum of comfort. The next action of the friends, when they finally meet Job, is the tearing of their garments by which they show solidarity with Job who had also torn his garments in his distress. Then the strange rite of throwing dust on themselves may have broadly the same implication of bonding with Job. Finally their taking the same posture as Job, sitting with him on the ground, for seven days and seven nights, can leave the reader (and Job) in no doubt that the friends did really come to share his grief. Whatever may come later in the poem cannot take away from the total bonding of the friends with Job in his sorrow in the Prologue.

One suggestion that may be helpful in interpreting the phrase 'they did not speak a word to (Hb *ĕl*) him' is that the proposition *ĕl*, nearly always, I think, as far as 2:13 goes, translated 'to', may also be translated 'about', 'concerning', thus giving the sense that while the friends, in their lamentation, did address Job, they made no comment concerning his misfortune from the religious point of view. By the time the friends arrive on the scene all the main characters have already spoken concerning Job from the religious point of view – the Lord praising Job's piety, and Satan questioning it, Job's wife advising her husband, while Job continues to praise God.

The friends alone keep silent on what is, after all, the central interest of the story: how should an innocent man relate to God in the midst of his sufferings? Yet they did not speak a word concerning Job from this point of view.

There are two situations when a good person may be tempted to turn against God: when he sees the success of the wicked or the humiliation of the just. Keeping silence when confronted with either of those two situations is an indication of how difficult theodicy is in real life.

In this context Psalm 39:1 may be quoted for a silence resulting not from having nothing to say, but from having too much to say:

> I said 'I will guard my ways,
> taking care not to sin with my tongue.
> I will put a muzzle in my mouth
> as long as the wicked are before me'.

As P. C. Craigie (*Psalms 1-50*, Waco, 1983, page 308), from whom the above translation is taken, comments: 'The psalmist's silence is determined by his fear that in his anger he might say something evil about God.' Job's wife, according to the LXX, spoke only after a long time had elapsed. Eliphaz, in the poem, also shows considerable hesitation in speaking, in case he might offend Job (4:2).

Job himself (in the poem, but not in the prose) eventually speaks harsh words about God only after having held back for some time:

> But I will not hold my peace; I will speak out in the distress of my mind (7:11).

And when Elihu begins to speak, he makes it clear that he does so only after he had held his peace for a long time in deference to the seniority of the three friends (32:4-6).

The silence of the three friends (2:13) may well have been inspired by the fear that by speaking out they would 'sin with their lips', and criticise God's ways with Job, because they were appalled at the extent of his sufferings. In this case their silence would be similar to that of the Psalmist (Ps 39).

The silence of the friends therefore was reprehensible in the sense that they did not bless God as Job had done. And this may well be the point of the Lord's reproach to them in 42:7, 8 in the famous 'repetition' clause:

> you have *not spoken* concerning me what is right as my servant Job has done (42:7, 8).

This is usually presumed to mean that the friends *had spoken* some words that were 'not correct' but, if we look again at the text, such a meaning does not impose itself. What the text says is negative not positive; it says they *didn't speak* what was correct, not that they spoke what was 'not correct'. The Lord said: 'I am angry with you ... because you have *not spoken* about me what is correct (*nᵉkhonah*)' (42:7).

What many commentators do is to take the negative *lo'* ('not') away from the verb *dibbartem* ('spoken') and join to it *nᵉkhonah* ('correct'), and end up with a positive verb followed by negative noun. While such a re-arrangement is possible, it is by no means necessary, and the original text may well be interpreted as indicating that the friends remained silent – 'they did not speak' – when the Lord would have preferred them to have spoken correctly of him as Job and done.

The danger of silence. The children of Job had not spoken a word against God, and still their father offered sacrifice just in case they blasphemed mentally (1:5). The Prologue-Epilogue moves in a world where even silence can be dangerous. When Job's three friends arrived on the scene of his sorrows, 'they raised their voices and wept' but they did not speak a word, and their silence lasted seven days. They expressed no religious attitude to the tragedy of Job – neither against God (as Job's wife may have done) nor in favour of God (as Job himself did). Could it be that their very silence, their failure to bless God, as Job had done, is the reason for the divine reproach (43:7)? Perhaps when 'they saw that his agony was very great' (2:13), they just could not honestly praise the Lord 'for all the evil he had inflicted on Job' (see 42:11 and 2:11).

We may note how important the term 'evil' is for the author of
the Prologue-Epilogue. He uses it seven times,[3] although most
translators avail themselves of synonyms – perhaps unwisely,
because our author has a rich vocabulary on this theme, if he wishes
to use it. The narrator, by the studied repetition of this word con-
trasts Job's 'turning from evil' (1:1, 8; 2:3) with the Lord's inflicting
evil on Job (2:10, see also 2:7). And when the friends hear 'of all this
evil' (2:11) they decide to visit Job. Finally, his relatives comfort him
'for all the evil the Lord had brought upon him' (42:11). Job, as he
said in the poem, looked for good, and evil came (30:26). How can
anyone praise God for inflicting evil on a good man? This may well
have been the unexpressed thought of the friends who kept silent
when faced with 'all this evil' which the Lord inflicted on Job. The
author also may be skilfully suggesting a similar thought by his
seven-fold use of the word 'evil', and also by putting the very
strong word $n^e bhalah$ on the lips of Yahweh in 42:8 when he asks Job
to pray for the friends 'so that I may not do anything *rash*' – the
same term used to describe the advice of Job's wife (2:10).[4] By his
skillful employment of such terms, the author of the prose is indicating his own critical approach to theodicy in a way which parallels
that taken by the angry Job of the poem. The patient Job of the prose
always speaks respectfully of God. The friends however remain
silent.

And for this silence they incurred the wrath of the Lord. In the
Prologue-Epilogue we are in the midst of a mythological scene
where the deity is portrayed in a far from edifying manner: a deity
who allows himself to be incited against a good man (Job) 'to
destroy him without cause' (2:3), and where all Job's children can
be wiped out as part of the testing of their father. Verse 7 of chapter
42 belongs to this 'long ago of mythology' in which the anger of the
deity is sometimes capricious, very different from the mature theology of the divine speech where no such anthropopathisms appear.

Still on this point of the Lord's condemnation of the friends in
42:7 (Epilogue): 'you have not spoken well of me': There is not one
verse in the poem to which anyone can point in support of this condemnation. The friends never utter a word against God; they do
utter words against Job, but not against God. Job, of course, accuses
the friends of speaking falsely in favour of God, in being partial
towards God, in taking God's side against him (13:7, 8). But is Job
correct in making this accusation? How can we assume that Job is
fairly stating his opponent's state of conscience? Are exegetes to
become partisan, taking Job's side against his friends? Only in the

Prologue can we point to a possible ground for their condemnation, viz. their not speaking what is right about the Lord as Job had done.

And when Job speaks in the poem about the Almighty's action in nature 'he selects examples illustrating God's unlimited and even irresponsible and destructive powers, whereas the friends emphasise the beneficent aspects of nature' (Driver-Gray, *Job*, Edinburgh 1921, 228). The clause saying that the friends 'have not spoken well of the Lord, as Job has done' makes no sense in the context of the poem, but only in the context of the prose legend.

This way of not linking the Lord's rebuke of the friends (42:7, 8) to anything they said in the poem finds only a few supporters, the most distinguished perhaps being Albrecht Alt, who felt obliged to posit some remarks by the friends in the hypothetical original prose legend behind our present Prologue, in which the friends would have urged Job to 'curse God and die' just as Job's wife is supposed to have done (2:9). The position which I have adopted doesn't need any hypothetical additions to the present text of the Prologue, but simply interprets their silence (2:13) in the light of the Lord's rebuke to them for 'not having spoken about him as Job did' (42:7, 8).

The offending clause (42:7b, 8b), brief as it is, gathers into itself the three most significant motifs of the Prologue:

> 1) The Lord's conferring on Job the highest encomium: 'my servant', which occurs nowhere else in the book except in the Prologue (It is also used in the Old Testament of Moses, the prophets, the patriarchs).
>
> 2) The Lord's acceptance of Job's response to his sufferings in which Job 'spoke what is right about me'.
>
> 3) And finally the failure of the friends, confronted with the sight of Job's misfortune, to speak of God as Job had done: 'you have not spoken what is right concerning me' (42:7 compare with 2:13).

Thus in one short clause (42:7b) in the Epilogue, the author is drawing us back to the Prologue. And the same cunning hand is at work once more.

The repetition is deliberate, and not the careless slip of an author whose hand and mind tires as he writes the final sentences of his long book. In the original legend in which the present Epilogue would have presumably followed very closely, if not immediately, the Prologue, such a repetition would have been otiose.

If we join together the last scene of the Prologue with the first scene of the Epilogue we get a well-rounded narrative unit (2:13; 42:7-10) which integrates well into the rest of the Prologue-Epilogue.

This unit consists of two scenes: in the first scene we get the journey of the three friends from their respective houses after they had heard of Job's misfortune, their arranging to come to visit Job for the purpose of sharing his sorrow with him and of comforting him. Then, on seeing him from afar, their dismay at his appearance; then their expression of their sorrow in loud lamentation and other acts of mourning, and finally their joining with him in his posture of grief, sitting next to him on the ground. The first scene concludes with the information that none of the friends 'spoke a word concerning him, for they saw that his grief was very great' (2:13).

The second scene then opens with the words presently found in the Epilogue (42:7): '(And it came to pass after the Lord had spoken these words *concerning* Job)'[5] the Lord said to Eliphaz, the Temanite, 'My anger is hot against you, and against your two friends because ye have not spoken *concerning* me what is correct, as my servant Job has done. 42:8: And now, take seven bullocks and seven rams, and go to my servant Job, and offer up a burnt offering on behalf of yourselves, and let my servant Job intercede for you; because I will accept him so that I deal not rashly with you; because ye have not spoken *concerning* me what is right as my servant Job has done' (my translation and italics).

One word on this translation: in the verses just quoted the preposition *'el* in conjunction with the verb *dibber* (to speak) occurs three times – I have italicised these for the benefit of the reader, and I have translated it by 'concerning' in all three instances. All translations I know use 'concerning' only in the two final instances, where the context make it unavoidable, but not in the first, even though, grammatically, all instances would permit 'concerning'.

How one translates this preposition makes a big difference to the whole meaning of the verses concerned. Thus, on 2:13, which, as generally translated, states that the friends did not speak a word to Job, I would make the following comment: The friends, in 'raising their voices' and 'weeping' for Job almost certainly spoke words of lamentation to comfort him, as articulate speech was part of lamentation. We get examples in the Keret legend of Keret's son and his daughter 'uttering their voices and weeping' followed immediately by the words they spoke to him. To say that the friends, who showed their grief for Job by sharing his posture of sorrow on the ground, didn't say anything at all to him for seven days hardly makes sense in the context of their 'lifting up their voices' and 'weeping' (*bkh*) for him. This fact suggests that we might explore the other possible translation for the preposition *'el*, viz. that the friends did not express any opinion concerning Job from the religious standpoint: should they curse God or should they bless God?

And in regard to 42:7 the same preposition is generally translated 'to': 'after the Lord had spoken these words *to* Job', which would automatically refer 'these words' to the *poem* (in which the Lord spoke to Job), and not to the *prose* (in which the Lord never speaks to Job but only *about* him). If however we translate *ʾel* as 'concerning', 'about', we then get the sense that after the Lord had spoken concerning Job (as he did twice in the Prologue, praising him) then he said to Eliphaz that he was angry with him and his two friends for not speaking properly of God, as Job had done.

The Lord, who had already spoken concerning the piety of his servant Job who had spoken so well of the Lord even in adversity, now declares that he is angry with the friends because they have not spoken of the Lord as Job had done. To avert his anger the Lord requires they offer sacrifices and that Job intercede for them. After Job has carried out his intercessory role, the Lord restores the fortunes of Job (and, according to the LXX, forgives the friends).

And so the real drama of Job has come to an end. Chapter 42 shows Job acting as a mediator acceptable to God, thus introducing a motif that was present in the extra-biblical lore about the three great exemplars of piety, Noah, Daniel and Job (mentioned by Ezechiel, 14:14-20) whose intercession might have been effective in Ezechiel's day if the land had not been so completely sinful. It is likely that this motif was present in the legend of Job of which the author and his audience would have been aware.

After this comes a brief scene of transition (42:11): all Job's brothers and sisters came to show their grief for him and to comfort him. Many scholars are rather dismissive of this scene: 'the concern of the relatives seems anticlimactic and unnecessary' (N. Habel); 'they kept away when he needed friends (19:13) and now they come along to accept his hospitality' (Driver-Gray). But the biblical author gives no indication of tongue in cheek. After the cruel death of his children for whom he had frequently offered sacrifice there was no quick return to joy for Job. And we may note that the cunning hand of the author introduces the word 'evil' for the seventh time in this verse. The relatives comfort Job 'for all the evil the Lord had brought upon him'. Job may have been totally patient with God's strange ways but the narrator is deliberately highlighting the evil that the Lord inflicted on Job who himself had always refrained from evil (1:1). And Job had been so deeply wounded by all the evil inflicted upon him that, like a survivor of the holocaust, he still needed to grieve (for his dead children and his own wounds) and to be comforted.

Finally comes the short section (42:12-17) which describes the 'last part' (*Aharith*) just as the preface (1:1-5) described 'the first part' (*re'shith*) of Job's life. After the turmoil and drama of the testing of Job we are back to tranquillity again. Family life, the birth of sons and beautiful daughters, the latter with fragrant names,[6] and Job's increased possessions. The narrator alone speaks to us in this Epilogue just as he did in the preface. He has told his story and brought it to a happy ending. His other, darker thoughts he reserves for the long poem, whose ending is far from 'happy'.

Conclusion

When the author of the Book of Job came at last to write the Epilogue he decided, I suggest, to compose a conclusion to his book that would operate at two different levels of intentionality. Firstly, the very proximity of the Epilogue to the great poem would ensure that readers would understand the Lord's rebuke to the friends to refer to what the friends had said in the poem. But a second intentionality also presents itself: the Epilogue has so many 'binders' with the Prologue, in vocabulary particularly, that readers could interpret the Lord's condemnation of the friends by referring it to their silence on an occasion when they ought to have praised God, but failed to do so because they were so appalled at the Lord's severity with Job.

To achieve this unique *double entendre* the author made skilful use of the ambiguity of the preposition *'el* in the opening clause of 42:7: 'And it came to pass after the Lord had spoken these things *'el* Job', which can refer to what the Lord spoke *to* Job (in the poem) or *concerning* Job (in the Prologue). See Brown Driver Briggs (*Lexicon*, 41a) on this point. Paul Joüon, in his *Grammaire de l'Hebreu Biblique* (Rome, 1947, par 133b), observes that it is *'el* one finds written instead of the expected *'al*, and attributes this confusion to copyists speaking the Aramaic language in which the preposition *'el* does not exist, and in which *'al* has all the meanings of the Hebrew *'el*. And since the copyists would pronounce the letter *'ayin* in a very feeble fashion, the confusion would be made all the easier.

Our biblical author, whose exotic language is 'loaded with Aramaisms and Arabisms' (Moshe Greenberg's phrase),[7] took advantage of such linguistic ambiguities to produce a conclusion which would satisfy the simple piety of that section of his readership whose faith needed a happy ending to the whole book, but which would also satisfy the more sophisticated sages who noticed that two different Jobs, with different temperaments and destinies, were being presented side by side, and that the happy ending of the naïve folktale was a far cry from the strong realism of the poem, in which, at the end, Job admits he has spoken 'things he did not understand' concerning the strange ways of the Creator, and is still in dust and ashes at the end of the poem (42:1-6), cleansed of his pride but not of his reason, nor indeed of his suffering.

The hand that wrote the Epilogue may indeed have departed from the literary grace of the Prologue, but that hand has not lost its cunning in 42:7, 8. By the deliberate employment of repetitions and of the ambiguous preposition 'el, it brings to a close two distinct stories, each still preserving its distinctive intentionality.

The bipolarity in the Book of Job is well summed up by David J. A. Clines in his recent commentary:[8] 'By all means let the patient Job be your model so long as that is possible for you; but if equanimity fails, let the grief and anger of Job the impatient direct itself and yourself toward God, for only in encounter with him will the tension of suffering be resolved.' Rarely has an exegete succeeded in saying so fairly in one short sentence what a large book is about.

Notes:

1. Kundera, Milan, *The Art of the Novel* (London, 1990) 146
2. Gibson, J. C. L., *Canaanite Myths and Legends* (Edinburgh, 1978) 95-97 from whose translation I have quoted the Keret text.
3. The word *ra'* three times in the sense of moral evil (1:1, 8; 2:3), and twice in the sense of physical evil (2:7; and 2:10 with the definite article); the term *raḁ* twice in the sense of physical evil (2:11; 'all this evil', and 42:11 'all the evil').
4. 'Some critics find this word ('rash') objectionable as applied to God's action since in common use it designates grave and wanton sin. It would be folly to amend this striking anthropopathism.' M. Pope, *Job*, New York, 1965, 350,'4.
5. In its present position in the Book of Job this clause is ambiguous: it may refer to what the Lord said *to* Job (in the poem), or to what the Lord said *concerning* Job (in the Prologue). Such is the sensitivity of the theological issues involved that the author may have deliberately availed himself of the ambiguity of the preposition 'el.
If, however, 4:7-10 is read as a continuation of 2:13, as I have been suggesting, the clause becomes superfluous but not unintelligible. In its present position after the poem it serves as a necessary jointure between poem and legend.

6. See on this seemingly 'irrelevant particularity' the Appendix 'The Keret Legend and the Prologue Epilogue of Job'.

7. Greenberg, Moshe, 'Job', in *The Literary Guide to the Bible* (London, 1987), 283.

8. Clines, David J. A., *Job*, Word Biblical Commentary, Dallas 1989, xxxix.

The Keret Legend
and the Prologue-Epilogue of Job

Among the cuneiform documents found between 1929-1939 at the ancient site of Ugarit on the north coast of Syria, one poem contains the legend of Keret, king of a place called Khubur. When G. R. Driver published his translation of the Keret poem in his *Canaanite Myths and Legends*,[1] he noted the similarity between the opening scenes of Keret and Job, when both men lament the loss of their property and children (p 5). There are, however, several other significant similarities between the Keret poem and the prose Prologue-Epilogue of Job which would support the hypothesis that an ancient folk-tale lies behind the Prologue-Epilogue of Job. The following list of parallels may be noted:

(1) Both Job, who was 'the greatest man in all the East' (1:3), and Keret, legendary king of Khubur, stood at the top of their respective hierarchies.

(2) Both are acknowledged by their god as good men. Of Job the Lord says that there is no one like him in all the earth, 'a man of blameless and upright life' (1:8); the supreme god of the Urgaritic pantheon, El, calls Keret 'the good one', or 'the gracious one' (Keret, 1, i, 40).[2] The emphasis on the high moral and religious character of both Keret and Job is maintained right through.

(3) Both heroes are afflicted by the death of all their children (Job 1:19; Keret l, i, 10-25).

(4) Both are stricken with personal illness. Job with running sores from head to foot (2:7). Keret is so seriously ill for over three months that his daughter thinks he's going to die (Keret II, ii, 35-50), and lifts up her voice in weeping for him (just as the friends of Job 'lifted up their voices and wept for him').

(5) Both Job and Keret are, however, accused of having neglected the poor, the widow and the orphan. This accusation is made, not by the deity, but by Job's friend Eliphaz (22:6-9) on one hand, and Keret's son and heir Yassib on the other (K II, vi, 25-53). The accusation is angrily rejected by both. The reader is never sure how true this accusation is. Yassib points out that his father's long illness

has reduced his supervision of the administration of justice within the realm, and that abuses have taken place through the old man's negligence. He says to his father: you are brother to a bed of sickness, friend to a bed of plague (K, II, vi, 51, 52).

G. R. Driver noted the similarity of this Ugaritic idiom with that used in Job's words: 'I called out to the pit "My father", and to the worm 'my mother and my sister' (Job 17:14).3 The son's charge, of course, may be tainted by his desire to take over from his father.

What is remarkable is that Job's friends admire him for the many good things he has done, how he once encouraged others who faltered and upheld the stumblers and the weak-kneed (Job 4:3, 4) but they still feel he has, perhaps unwittingly, fallen into evil ways. Eliphaz, in his first two speeches, never mentions any specific sin of Job's, but in his third and final speech he specifically mentions Job's harsh treatment of a poor kinsman, the widow and the orphan (22:6-9). The suggestion of some scholars that the friends 'invented' the sins of Job in order to safeguard God's justice at any cost finds no support except in Job's own counter-attack on the friends.

One of the most striking parallels is that both Job and Keret after their long illness are restored to health once more (Job 42:10; Keret II, vi, 10-15).

(6) To crown this happy ending we find that both Job and Keret, whose children were wiped out at the beginning of their respective stories, are now finally blessed with a new family: Job with seven sons and three beautiful daughters (42:13); Keret with a new wife who bears him seven sons and at least six daughters (Keret III, iii, 5-12). An extraordinary parallel emerges in the manner of giving the names of all the daughters, but not of the sons. The names of Job's three daughters are given (42:14). In the epic *Ba al and Anat* (also from Ugarit) their three daughters are named, but not the sons. In the Keret poem there is no list of his sons by their names, but when it comes to the birth of the daughters we get six parallel lines, short lines of only three words each, but the final word in each gave the name of the girl. Unfortunately, only in the sixth line can the name of the (favourite) daughter of Keret be reconstructed; the text is damaged in the other five, but the space for the name was there.

When Driver-Gray, in their renowned *Commentary on Job* faulted the writer of the Epilogue for including the 'irrelevant particularity' of the names of Job's daughters, they underestimated the deep springs in ancient legend from which the author of the Prologue-Epilogue may have been drawing.

(7) In both the Keret poem and in the Prologue-Epilogue of Job

the assembly of the gods is an important mythological motif, and it takes place twice in each document. In all cases the heavenly council discusses the affairs of a human being of great distinction, Job and Keret, who are highly regarded by the deity, and both honoured by the title of 'the servant of god'. Keret is referred to twice as servant of God, *ebhed el* (I, iii, 49 and 51);4 and the Lord frequently speaks of 'my servant Job' (in Prologue and Epilogue – but never in the poem).

(8) Animal Sacrifices. Like Job, who first 'consecrated' his children (1:5) by ritual washings, before he offered sacrifices to expiate for the possible mental sins of which his grown children might, in their festivities, have been guilty, so we find Keret:

He washes himself …, washes his hands to the elbow …

He takes a lamb of sacrifice in his hands

… loaves of bread, the entrails of a bird of sacrifice (K, I, ii, 8-18).

Again in the epilogue, but not in the poem, we find reference to a very large animal-sacrifice in reparation for the friends' failure to speak well of God (42:7, 8).

All these similarities between the Keret legend and the Prologue-Epilogue of Job suggest the possibility that the author of the Job poem consciously drew on an ancient folk-tale of the Keret type in which the upright hero suffered loss of family and property, but was eventually restored to his former happiness. The patient Job of the Prologue-Epilogue, like Keret, never speaks against the deity, and in this is in total contrast to the impatient Job of the poem.

The Prologue-Epilogue of Job is a very short story consisting of only 45 verses, and to find that it shares several important elements of its narrative structures with the Keret legend from the library of Ugarit is highly suggestive of cultural influence.

One must acknowledge, however, that the whole intention of the Keret poem differs from that of the Prologue-Epilogue. The former is dominated by Keret's desire to replace his lost family and to secure the succession to the throne. The latter is concerned with the question whether Job will continue in his religious integrity even in adversity, while the poem of Job has a further problem to ponder, viz, how can innocent suffering be reconciled with the justice of God?

Even within the book of Job, then, we have two quite distinct problems: the prose Prologue-Epilogue presents the patient Job maintaining his piety in spite of his sufferings, whereas in the poem it is the impatient and angry Job who accuses God of being unjust in the moral governance of the world. The movement of thought from

Prologue to poem is thus not in one straight line of logical progression. In fact we get two lines, not one. The author in both prose and poetry is exploring the sufferings of the innocent, but in two separate directions. The author is an artist, not a systematic theologian, and the function of the artist, as Anton Chekhov said, is not to arrive at a solution to a problem but to present the problem properly. Our author explores a thesis in the prose (the patient Job), and an antithesis in the poem (the impatient Job), but never a synthesis. Writing as an artist of genius, he depicts the ideal in which the patient sufferer (of the prose) eventually is restored to happiness. But in his poem he depicts the real world of human sorrow and bitterness and unresolved questioning, where justice is not seen to be done. This dual portrayal of the ideal and the real lends majesty and scale to his study of Job's suffering, and presents the two approaches to the perennial agony of man. Into the edifying prose tale the poet has inserted his far-from-edifying poem of the fury of the afflicted Job against his God. And the piety of the prose serves to attenuate somewhat the harsh impiety of the poem, thereby rendering the whole book more acceptable to the religious community of Israel who eventually included it in their canon of scripture. An ancient Keret-type story may have inspired our author in fashioning the Prologue-Epilogue, and models from Sumer and from Babylon were at hand for the poem. The resulting book allows many voices to flow together into one of literature's greatest masterpieces.

Other matters on which differences emerge between the Keret story and the Prologue-Epilogue of Job are the high regard for women in Keret and the dismissive tone of Job. Keret's second wife Huray is praised not only for her beauty: 'her grace is as the grace of the goddess Anat', with special reference to her eyes 'like gems of sapphire' (K. I, vi, 25), but also for her concern for the needy, so much so that when she bade farewell to her father's royal house to become the wife of Keret, the people of the kingdom bemoaned the departure of their benefactress (K, III, i, 1-7). Her daughter Thitmanat was, in later years, so highly appreciated by her father Keret that, during his long illness, it was her comforting presence the king sought in preference to that of his son, whom he politely dismisses:

> Son, weep not, lament not for me; Call in thy sister Thitmanat, (my) daughter whose affection is strong; for I know that thy sister is full of compassion (K, II, 1, 25-35).

How different is Job's attitude to women. His reproach of his

wife for her irreverent advice to him is overly harsh, with its gener-
alised reference to 'foolish women' (2:10). Within the poem too Job
finds no consolation in his wife's attitude (19:17). There is not one
verse in the entire book of Job in which he speaks well of any
woman. Only at the very end does Job redeem himself from the
charge of anti-feminism by his decision to give his daughters 'an
inheritance with their brothers' (42: 15).[5]

Finally, when we come to the concept of God, we find in Keret
an elevated and refined appreciation of El, the chief god of the
Ugaritic pantheon. El, the father of gods and men, is benign,
patient, never angry. He is concerned for the welfare of Keret, and
when the other gods refuse his request to bring healing to Keret, El
himself arranges for his cure (K, II, v, 10-30). In all this El exhibits a
high moral standard not always followed by the lesser divinities of
his heavenly council. But, all in all, the Keret poem shows that the
ancient semitic civilization of Ugarit, which came to an end circa
1200 BC, expressed noble ideals in its religious and moral thinking.

The Prologue-Epilogue of Job, on the other hand, portrays a less
than perfect relationship between the Lord and humans, where the
supreme deity can allow himself to be 'incited' against a good man,
Job, 'to destroy him without cause' (2:3), and where all Job's children can be wiped out as part of a wager with Satan (1:19). A comment in the Talmud on verse 2:3 is sufficient: When Rabbi Johanan
reached this verse he wept, saying 'when it is possible to incite a
master against his servant, is there any hope?' Finally in 42:8, the
Lord's threatening language, 'my anger is hot against you', to the
friends uses the strongest possible expression: he asks that Job
should pray for the friends 'so that I may not do anything rash' ($n^e b$-
$halah$ – a very strong word, which many commentators find blasphemous, since it implies that the Lord could easily do something
immoral he would afterwards be ashamed of). The author of the
Prologue-Epilogue portrays an ideally patient man (Job), but his
portrayal of God falls short of what later revelation will bring. It
also falls short of what the poet of Ugarit thought about the
supreme deity. Another significant ideological difference between
Keret and Job concerns the idea of sacral kingship so important in
ancient Near Eastern belief, of which Keret, but not Job, is an example! The belief that the king is the channel of divine blessing to his
people, and that if he suffers so do they, and if he prospers they
share his well-being.[6]

If the author of Job drew on a Keret-type story, he was selective
in his use of it, as indeed was his right. Nevertheless the similarities

between the Keret legend and the Prologue-Epilogue of Job are considerable, especially in the narrative structures. Both have the opening scene with the hero fallen from his high position through the loss of family and property. Both men are the subject of the deliberations of the heavenly council, and are highly regarded by the supreme deity. In addition to the loss of family and property both suffer serious bodily illness over a long period bringing them close to death. Both are consoled in their sorrows by friends: Job's friends arranged to come 'to condole with him and comfort him . . . and they wept for him' when they saw how deteriorated his appearance was (Job 2:11, 12). Keret's son and his daughter also weep and lament for him and comment on his appearance: 'thy looks are passed away like a dog's' (K, II, i, 15, 16). Then, both Job and Keret are criticised for their neglect of the poor; this criticism, however, is never made against Job in the Prologue-Epilogue, but only in the poem. Again, there is no harsh word spoken against the deity in Keret nor by Job in the Prologue-Epilogue. Both heroes are eventually restored to health, and both are blessed with new families of sons and daughters, with the seemingly 'irrelevant particularity' of the listing of the girls' names.

In the Prologue of Job Satan enters a meeting of the heavenly assembly and accuses Job of being motivated by self-interest. The figure of Satan acting as an accuser, or prosecuting attorney, at the heavenly court in cases concerning humans, is also found in Zechariah 3:1, where the high priest Joshua is seen in a dream 'and Satan standing at his right hand to accuse him'. In this later scene, however, the Lord rebukes Satan, whereas in Job the Lord permits Satan to inflict great evils on the innocent Job. In the Hebrew Bible the figure of Satan is generally that of the accuser, but in Job he is not merely an accuser but also the one who brings evil on the innocent. In this respect the Book of Job has a close resemblance to the Ugaritic literature which does not use the term Satan, but does, nevertheless, have a member of the heavenly council who both accuses and smites the innocent.

The clearest example from Ugarit is afforded by the Aqhat poem, also referred to as the Danel poem from the name of the ancient worthy Danel (the father of Aqhat).

Danel's son Aqhat refused to give his warrior's bow to the violent goddess Anat, who then, like Satan in Job, accuses Aqhat before the supreme deity El and also receives authorisation from El to smite the young Aqhat, something she does with terrible consequences, ending unintentionally, it seems, in his death. The parallel with Satan's smiting of Job almost to the point of death is very clear, including the detail that Job's children and Aqhat were killed during a meal.

In view of the danger of excessive force in this case we can appreciate how timely was the Lord's restraining command to Satan, 'but spare his (Job's) life' (Job 2:6).

If we turn now to the Keret legend, we find two accusations made against him. One, already mentioned, is made by his son Yassib, and concerns his neglect of the poor; the other is with regard to his failure to fulfil his vow – a failure to give the goddess of Tyre her due offerings. We may note that Job is also accused of two different kinds of offence: neglect of the poor (by Eliphaz 22:6-9), and a piety motivated by self-interest (1:9).

The whole mythological atmosphere of the Ugarit poems and the Prologue-Epilogue of Job is remarkably similar. The true cultural homeland for the prose of Job is likely to be the stretch of coastline from Ugarit to Tyre and Sidon, touching the northern borders of Israel, and linked together from Solomonic times down to the ninth century BC when Jezebel, princess of Phoenicia, married Ahab, the king of Israel, and undoubtedly brought the religious poems and the myths, and the story of the fury of the goddess Athirat (Asherah), with her.

Notes:
1. Edinburgh, 1965.
2. I am using G. R. Driver's sigla throughout.
3. Ugaritica, VI (Paris, 1969), 184
4. Another term used in the Keret legend is *glm*, which may be translated 'lad' (C H. Gordan), 'servitor' (G. R. Driver), 'page' (J. C. L. Gibson), in the sense of page-boy to the god El. See *Ugaritic Handbook* by C. H. Gordan (Rome, 1947) sub voce. The king is, thus, the loyal servant of El. He is also his progeny, but this latter theologumenon from the royal ideology of Ugarit finds no echo in the Book of Job.
5 A provision more generous than Israel's legislation on inheritance by daughters when there are sons.
6. See G. R. Driver, *Canaanite Myths and Legends*, 2nd Edition (Edinburgh, 1978), 23 where J. C. L. Gibson makes this point.

Summary: The Epilogue
42:7-16

With the Epilogue we are back into prose once more, where the literary style and the vocabulary of the Prologue re-appear in all their theological naïvety. We may note especially the repetitions, e.g. 'my servant Job', in both Prologue and Epilogue.

The Prologue and the Epilogue taken together constitute an old folktale of an innocent sufferer who is eventually restored to health, a theme also found in other ancient civilisations, e.g. the Keret legend from Ugarit.

The Epilogue consists of two parts:

a) 42:7-10 The Lord commends Job for speaking well of him, and condemns the friends for their silence.

b) 42:11-17 The Lord restores Job to prosperity. He has a family as numerous as before. His three beautiful daughters get inheritance rights. After a long life Job dies.

(We search in vain in the Epilogue for any mention of the wife of Job. Is she the mother of the second family? And did Job recover from his own physical and mental ailments? The so-called 'happy ending' leaves many questions unanswered.)

Text: The Epilogue
42:7-21

42:7 After the Lord had spoken these words to (*or* concerning) Job, the Lord said unto Eliphaz the Temanite: 'My wrath is kindled against you and your two friends; for ye have not spoken that which is right concerning me as *my servant Job* has. 8 Now, therefore, take unto you seven bullocks and seven rams, and go unto *my servant Job*, and offer for yourselves a holocaust, and let *my servant Job* pray for you; for his plea will I accept, not to do anything rash to you. For ye have not spoken that which is right concerning me as *my servant Job* has.'

9 So Eliphaz the Temanite, and Bildad the Shuhite, and Sophar the Namaathite went and did as the Lord had commanded them; and the Lord accepted Job's plea. Then the Lord restored the fortunes of Job when he prayed for his friends; and the Lord doubled all of Job's possessions. Then all his brethren and all his sisters and all his former acquaintances came and ate bread with him in his house; and they condoled with him, and comforted him concerning all the evil which the Lord had brought upon him, and each one gave him a piece of money or a gold ring. 12 And the Lord blessed the latter end of Job more than the beginning; and he had fourteen thousand sheep, and six thousand camels, and a thousand yoke of oxen, and a thousand she-asses. 13 And he had seven sons and three daughters; and he called the name of the first Jemimah, and the name of the second Qesiah, and the name of the third Qerenhappuch. 15 And there were not found in all the land women as fair as the daughters of Job; and their father gave them inheritance among their brethren.

16 And after this, Job lived one hundred and forty years, and saw his children and his children's children, four generations. 17 And so Job died, old and full of days.

The Triune God
A BIBLICAL, HISTORICAL AND THEOLOGICAL STUDY
Thomas Marsh

This book offers a study of the theology of the Trinity from its origin in biblical history, through the significant periods of its history down the centuries, to the state of this theology at the present time. It is a comprehensive overview of the subject, a study in breadth rather than in depth, whose primary aim is to satisfy the needs of students and others who seek a general presentation of the topic, rather than specialised discussion of some of its particular aspects.

The chapters are:
1. The God of Israel
2. The God of Early Christianity
3. The First Theology: Before Nicaea
4. The Great Controversy
5. The Latin tradition and Scholastic theology
6. Theology of the Trinity today

Thomas A. Marsh was Professor of Dogmatic Theology at St Patrick's College, Maynooth, until his death in 1994.

1 85607 106 5   208pp   £9.99

Greek Philosophy and the Christian Notion of God

Gerard Watson

Greek philosophy had formed the minds of the educated classes of the Roman Empire for centuries before the early Christians set out to spread their message there. If they wished to gain a hearing, therefore, the language of Greek philosophy was the language they had to speak. This venture was to have a long history and an enduring effect both upon Christianity itself and on the world which it was seeking to convince and convert. This book is about the impact of Greek philosophy, from Plato and Aristotle through to Neoplatonism, on Christian thinkers down to medieval scholasticism and St Thomas Aquinas. Using the excellent studies already available, such as those by Jaeger and others, but always working from the original texts and sources, Gerard Watson charts and follows the deepening involvement of Christian thought with this other form of discourse until, as he says, 'the philosophers themselves become Christian'.

Gerard Watson is Professor of Ancient Classics at St Patrick's College, Maynooth.

1 85607 112 X   160pp   £8.99

Iníon Mhaor an Uachta

DRÁMA

Breandán Ó Doibhlin

Dráma thrí ngníomh é seo atá suite le linn Phlandáil Chúige Uladh, díreach roimh Éirí Amach 1641. Tá an choimhlint ag géarú idir Protastúnachas agus Caitliceachas, agus an cultúr dúchais sáinnithe i lár baill. Insítear mar a cuireadh ceann de shéadchomharthaí an chultúir sin ó bhaol, Clog Naomh Pádraig, atá anois in Ard-Mhusaem na hÉireann. Iniúchadh atá sa dráma ar fhréamhacha an fhoréigin i gCúige Uladh, ar an choibhneas idir chreideamh, cultúr, polaitíocht agus fainiceacht.

This is a three-act play set during the Plantation of Ulster, just before the 1641 Rising. Conflict between Protestantism and Catholicism is sharpening up, and the native culture is caught in the middle. It tells how one of the great national treasures, St Patrick's Bell which is now in the National Museum, was kept safe during the conflict. This play won the Abbey Theatre award for plays in Irish in 1993.

Breandán Ó Doibhlin is Professor of French at St Patrick's College, Maynooth.

1 85607 109 X   80pp   £4.99

You Are Mine

A VIEW OF THE SPIRITUAL LIFE

Myles Rearden CM

Fr Myles Rearden is Spiritual Director at St Patrick's College, Maynooth. He worked for many years in Africa and has taken internships in Spiritual Direction in the United States. In this book he explores the variety of spiritual living, while giving it some clarity of focus by presenting his own experience of a growing relationship with God within the Vincentian tradition. He presents spiritual living as a growth process, and an arduous one at that.

The opening chapters anchor spiritual growth in the experience of individual people, of the church, and of various cultural groups. Chapters four and five speak of how people grow spiritually during their lives. Chapter six deals with ways to grow spiritually, seven with spiritual growth that begins with a condition of addiction, and eight with the completion of spiritual growth in and after a person's death.

Myles Rearden CM is Spiritual Director at St Patrick's College, Maynooth.

1 85607 105 7   144pp   £8.99

Literature and the Supernatural

Edited by Brian Cosgrove

Julia Kristeva has claimed that modernity can be characterised as 'the first epoch in human history in which human beings attempt to live without religion'. Does this mean then that 'supernatural' is also well-nigh defunct as a category? This collection of essays, by members of the English Department in Maynooth, considers the manifestations of the supernatural (or supra-natural) not just in modern works but in earlier writings from medieval times and from the nineteenth century. The variety of topics is matched by a diversity of approach: the result is a kaleidoscopic presentation in which the supernatural, broadly defined, is considered either directly or obliquely as it offers itself for documentation, analysis and critique in literature, cultural history and film.

Brian Cosgrove is Professor and Head of the English Department at St Patrick's College, Maynooth.

ISBN 1 85607 143 X   176pp   £9.99

Anglo-Irish Poems
of the Middle Ages

Edited by Angela M. Lucas

The English poems of the British Library Manuscript, Harley 913, were written in Ireland in the early fourteenth century. The manuscripts have strong Franciscan associations. Sometimes called 'The Kildare Poems', both because of their association with that area and because one of them claims to have been written by Friar Michael of Kildare, the poems show considerable influences of the Irish culture in which they were cradled. They are also full of ideas, themes, and images which are part of the Western European Christian tradition and especially close in affinity to the acknowledged works of Franciscan friars. They are a unique witness to English literature in Ireland at this period.

This edition has been prepared with an introduction on the manuscript and language. Each poem has a facing-page translation and a commentary. There is also a bibliography.

Angela M. Lucas is a Lecturer in English at St Patrick's College, Maynooth, teaching Medieval English.

ISBN 1 85607 142 1   224pp   £10.99